Let The Seller Beware

Let The Seller Beware

by
James Bishop, Jr.
and
Henry W. Hubbard

Introduction by Betty Furness

THE NATIONAL PRESS INC.
128 C STREET, NORTHEAST
WASHINGTON, D.C. 20002

Acknowledgments

A great many people contributed to this book, from *Newsweek's* Washington Bureau Chief Mel Elfin, who encouraged us to write it and pushed us to finish it, to *Newsweek's* editors who tolerated our occasional absences during an incredibly eventful year.

Among those who helped immeasurably were, Senate Commerce Committee counsel Michael Pertschuk; Betty Furness; Ralph Nader; Leslie Dix, Director for Legislative Affairs, President's Committee on Consumer Interests; The Better Business Bureaus; the American Advertising Federation; Paul Rand Dixon, Chairman of the Federal Trade Commission; FTC Commissioner Mary Gardiner Jones; Melvin Belli; Jerry Sonosky; Newsweek Librarian Ted Slate; Geraldine Carro; Senator Warren Magnuson and all the girls in the Washington Bureau.

Most of all, we thank Caroline Bishop and Jean Hubbard, our editors and typists, and happily, still our wives.

Contents

Introduction

A hundred years ago, the concept of the consumer did not exist in America. The range of goods available was narrow, and the list of a family's needs was basic. The relationship between buyer and seller were personal and direct. The simplicity of the marketplace provided little room for abuse.

As our economy grew from agrarian to industrial, the way of life of the average American changed dramatically. Technological progress brought man marvels never dreamed of, but it also brought confusion and perils he could not have foreseen. An imbalance was created in the marketplace, and society was slow to correct it.

It was not until well after the turn of this century that President Theodore Roosevelt was able to claim that America had awakened to the fact that "no man may poison the public for his private profit." But even then, the bold statement was ahead of its time. Free enterprise was freely translated to mean *caveat emptor*—let the buyer beware—and there was a tacit acceptance of the principle that anything a merchant could get away with was acceptable.

Only recently have Americans realized that this doctrine erodes our traditional concept of justice. They have wearied of feeling victimized by merchants and manufactures, and they have set out to reform and rectify the balance between buyer and seller.

Consumers are not professional lobbyists in pursuit of personal gain; they are 200 million amateurs in pursuit of fair play.

The past five years have seen the greatest surge of consumer legislation in the history of this country. Opponents of this legislation have called it meddlesome. I don't think it is meddlesome to guarantee a housewife that the meat she serves her family is not diseased, or that the toys she buys for her children are not poisonous or liable to burst into flame.

I don't think it is meddlesome to force a creditor to tell the borrower how much interest he will have to pay on a loan. It is just common sense.

That is what the consumer "revolution" is all about. It is a revolution toward reason and common sense and justice.

Informed and alert consumers are the greatest defenders of the free enterprise system. The government's role must be as provider of the tools the consumer needs to achieve justice and recourse. As the representative of the people, the government must define consumer ethic, and must act as arbiter and adjudicator.

I think Messrs. Bishop and Hubbard have performed a valuable public service with "Let The Seller Beware." They point up the justice of the consumer cause. They stress the importance of morality in the marketplace—the same morality on which our free enterprise system is based. The book is not simply an angry catalogue of abuses. It perceptively analyzes the history of the consumer movement in America, examining the progress made so far and detailing the problems that will impress on all Americans the dangers that can be spawned by lethargy, and the rewards that can be reaped from commitment.

Betty Furness
Special Assistant to
The President for Consumer
Affairs
November 1968

Author's Note

This book grew out of a *NEWSWEEK* cover story early this year on Ralph Nader. The story concerned itself mainly with Nader the man and his efforts to identify and correct the imbalances and inequities in the American marketplace.

As our research broadened it became clear that the term "consumerism," coined to describe both Nader's crusade and the new legislative push for consumer protection, involved considerably more than an occasional skirmish between government and industry over a deceptively advertised headache pill. The consumer revolt of the 1960's proved to be a far more complex phenomenon.

The rising expectations of millions of better educated American consumers is clashing with a slower rise in the reliability and quality of goods in the marketplace, unsatisfactory corporate disclosure and a deterioration in the quality of services.

At the same time, the American conscience is beginning to rebel against the debasement of the environment. These factors combined with strong White House leadership, have blended into a nonpartisan political force which looks beyond mere quantity in each man's life to the quality of his life.

The book therefore tells the story of a 60-year-long battle to outlaw the anachronistic doctrine of *caveat emptor*—let the buyer beware—that is just now beginning to succeed. But we also attempt to explain why the battle needed to be fought and why it should succeed, for the sake of government, industry and consumer alike.

James Bishop, Jr., Henry Hubbard
Washington, D.C., November 29, 1968

The Newest -ISM

chapter 1

It was 10 o'clock on the morning of April 29, 1968. The doors to room 3302 in the New Senate Office Building swung open and corporate overlords from General Motors, Ford, Chrysler and American Motors filed in past the guard, past crowded rows of lawyers and reporters and strode directly to their seats behind the witness table. Across the room, Senator Abraham Ribicoff of Connecticut sternly and impatiently called for quiet. An auto lobbyist leaned forward in his seat and whispered to a reporter: "Jesus, there's going to be a battle."

Almost two years after the regrettably bitter fight between the industry and government had ended with passage of the nation's first Federal traffic safety law, another confrontation seemed imminent. Senator Ribicoff had summoned the big four to ask them a simple question: does a shoulder-harness in a new auto cost $25.00 as the companies were saying, or $3.00, as their chief critic Ralph Nader had written in the *New Republic*? All the signs suggested that the industry was blaming a recent wave of price increases on the added cost of Federally-required safety features, and Senator Ribicoff deeply resented the apparent effort to make safety a scapegoat. He had, in fact, already introduced a bill which would require the true price of each safety device, from sideview mirrors to backup lights, to be stated on the bill of sale.

The first witness was GM executive vice president Richard Gerstenberg. It couldn't be done Ribicoff's way, he said. "A car has 14,000 separate parts," he protested. "They have no separate price identity." He respectfully doubted that the bill would be "meaningful to either the government or the public."

"Incredible!" bellowed Ribicoff. "I find it shocking that the most efficient industry in the world doesn't know what its costs and prices are." So it went through the morning, thrust and parry, the Senator's view of the public's right to know versus the executives' view of the right to keep their affairs private.

The audience settled back for one more dreary and depressing round in the classic battle between government and industry. But suddenly, after two hours of futile colloquy, the hearing took a dramatic turn. Ford president Arjay Miller conceded that the issue of safety costs was somewhat confusing. He then suggested that industry might sit down with government and work out an index of price information. Each company would submit its own cost figures. A government agency would then compute and publish an average cost for each item, but keep each company's specific, and carefully-guarded, cost data confidential. In this way, Miller suggested, both public and private interests could be served to the satisfaction of all.

An audible wave of astonishment swept the audience. Ribicoff was momentarily speechless. After the four companies had conferred and agreed on the plan, Ribicoff declared: "I like the idea better than mine." He adjourned the hearings.

What had happened? The issue was small by comparison to the more flaming consumer debates of the day, but the response of industry was significant beyond the purpose of the hearing. In the hallway later, Ribicoff offered an analysis. "Industry is developing a new public attitude," he declared happily. "Nothing like this could have happened a few years ago."

Ribicoff's words—one of the rare occasions when he has felt compelled to speak kindly of the industry—may have been just wishful thinking. It took the auto-makers many months to stop a highly questionable pricing practice, and when they did, they yielded on their own terms. That is admittedly the pessimistic interpretation, but it is one based solidly on the industry's abysmal insensitivity to the society around it in the past. But Senator Ribicoff might also be right. Times may be changing.

This is the Decade of the Consumer, and as bill after bill has been fought out and won for the consumer, industry has begun to heed the flashing amber light: a new social consciousness is demanded, and the forces demanding it now have the power to impose it on American industry. Auto safety, meat inspection, "truth-in-lending," gas-pipeline safety, all were bitterly resisted, but a strong law passed in each case. In short, *caveat venditor:* let the seller beware.

The fly-by-night operator, whose sole purpose is to cheat the consumer, operates outside the law. Through painful experience, the American consumer knows his style and does his best to shun his persuasive pitches. The American businessman is no less offended by the operations of the shysters, and has created such organizations as the Better Business Bureau and the American Federation of Advertising Agencies to help keep them out of the marketplace. But within the past decade, the disturbing realization has slowly come to the American consumer that unethical, antisocial, and amoral business practices are not confined to the fringes of the marketplace; they also exist at the core of the American economic system, daily practiced by the same respected giants of industry that made this nation the most powerful and affluent on earth.

It is largely true, and consoling, that the consumer's problems are not deliberately created for him by the U.S. corporate leaders. "They don't sit in locked rooms and talk about what they can do to be deceitful," says Betty Furness, Special Assistant to the President for Consumer Affairs. But after a year at her post, Miss Furness was obliged to report that serious problems existed nevertheless. "More things need watching than I was aware of," she said. "There is more fraud and deceit than I anticipated."

The trouble is not in the precepts of the American economy, but in its practices. No fundamental weakness in capitalism or the profit system has been identified, and none is suggested here. There can be no doubt that this nation's industrial revolution has created the most productive and rewarding economic system in history. But the robber barons who created it handed down as part of their legacy a system and an attitude with monstrous flaws. The ills they inflicted upon the society are such a part of the American scene that some, such as water and air pollution, may already be impossible to eliminate. Others are correctable, but the lengthy and often vicious battles over impure meat, dangerous drugs, or hidden installment costs amply demonstrate how difficult they are to identify, fix, and eliminate.

The modern businessman cannot be blamed for creating the industrial system. Nevertheless, he can be blamed for preserving it in its original form. He defends the status quo with all his strength, and warns that any change, any governmental intrusion, any adjustment not of his own making, will lead to disaster. To an extent, he is right. Wanton disregard of the realities of American business could seriously disrupt the nation's economy. Revolutionary schemes such as nationalization or decentralization could very well end in disaster. But such an attack has never been mounted or even intended.

It would not succeed if it were. For all its serious flaws, the system built by the Morgans and the Rockefellers at least has permanence. Indeed, the edifice created by the American industrial revolution has such structural rigidity that it has proved and is still proving to be incredibly resistant to change. But it is change that the consumerists want—not a revolution in economics, but a revolutionary change in the attitude of its practitioners.

Twice in history, the consumer has attempted to alter the system, once at the turn of the century and again after the Depression. The common-law doctrine of *caveat emptor*, based on the presumed equality between buyer and seller meeting face-to-face in the marketplace, had become outmoded as trade expanded and transportation made new markets available to distant producers. As the distance between buyer and seller grew, and the quality of their transactions became steadily more impersonal and irresponsible, the marketplace was on its way to becoming a vast twilight zone of danger, deception, and doubt.

Congress was more concerned with protecting the burgeoning American industry against itself than in protecting the consumer. The Sherman anti-trust act was designed to preserve "freedom of competition," while the Interstate Commerce Commission was established to prevent the transportation industry from cheating producers. The only true consumer bills passed Congress in 1906—the Pure Food and Drug Act and the Meat Inspection Act, which attempted to stem the tide of adulterated, misbranded and dangerous foods, patent medicines, and meat. Creation of the Federal Trade Commission and passage of the

Clayton anti-trust act in 1914 were indirectly of benefit to the average citizen, but again were designed primarily to protect the less rugged individualists trying to survive the rigors of *laissez-faire* economics. New Deal politics offered another opportunity for action in the public interest, but most of this second round of consumer reform was consumed in trying to resurrect the laws passed during the first round.

Each era of reform achieved few meaningful changes in operations in the marketplace. For each sharp practice that was proscribed, a dozen new ones took its place. Technology quickly outpaced legislation, and the courts often threw out Congress's laws as unwarranted intrusions on the rights of private property. Despite Presidential support in both eras, the political power that came to the support of the consumer was diffident and irregular. In the end, it was not the efforts of the consumerists that got any legislation passed, but outside help in the form of horror stories and poignant tragedies. In 1906, it was publication of *"The Jungle,"* by Upton Sinclair. His concern was directed toward the plight of the processors, and not the condition of the meat they processed, but the book turned so many stomachs that both the food and drug act and the hastily written meat inspection act passed Congress easily.

Again in 1933 another book graphically entitled *"100,000,000 Guinea Pigs"* got the movement rolling, but it was not until more than 100 people were killed by a patent medicine called *Elixir Sulfanilimide* that any new consumer legislation passed. These momentary waves of emotion were enough to carry some laws past the forces that opposed them, but not enough to sustain a movement—and not enough to effect any permanent change in the marketplace.

Now the United States is in the midst of a third round of consumer agitation. It had no exact beginning. A variety of concerns grew up independently among America's citizens, and eventually joined together to give the consumer movement a broadness and an urgency it had never before had. "There are times," J.K. Galbraith has said, "when all looks peaceful and much goes wrong." The 1950s were such a time. Signs of trouble appeared beneath the veneer of prosperity and affluence, touching the lives of everyone, threatening and chastening them. Twenty deaths in Donora, Pa., in 1948 from smog filled with toxic fumes from nearby metallurgical plants were shrugged off as a special case. But the 4,000 deaths in London in 1952 were no such special case; ordinary urban pollutants generated by the city's commerce and industry were the culprits, and citizens from New York to Los Angeles were advised by public health authorities that it could happen there, too. Each individual who grew up or raised a family in the fifties can no doubt remember being touched by a steady deterioration. "Polluted" signs popped up on favorite beaches. Soot appeared on the apartment windowsill and the shirtcollar. The rising lung cancer or traffic fatality rates reached a friend or relative. The prepackaged steak had a giant bone on its invisible side. Evidences large and small accumulated and finally became intolerable. The system itself laid the groundwork for the movement now unfolding—a movement not restricted to a few special concerns, not driven by a few emotional causes that will die out as they did before, but a movement that fused all its disparate complaints into an urgent concern for the quality of life itself. The cumulative effect has put American business on the defensive as it never has been before.

The tone of the era was set by the Kennedy administration. Arthur Schlesinger, Jr. summed up the young President's concern for society thusly in *A Thousand Days*:* ". . . Despite his support of economic growth and his concern over persisting privation, the thrust of his preoccupation was less with the economic machine and its quantitative results than with the quality of life in a society which in the main, had achieved abundance."

It was Kennedy's destiny never to possess the mandate from the public and the power over Congress to put much of his concern for the quality of life into effect. But he talked about it, and when he talked the nation listened and began to adopt his concerns. In 1962, Kennedy sent a special consumer message to Congress—the first ever. Though some 33 government agencies were then engaged in some form of consumer protection, the battle was an uneven one, and the President called for a

*Houghton Mifflin, New York, 1965.

reexamination of the relationships between manufacturer and consumer. The message also called for the consumer to be newly vested with four basic rights: the right to safety, the right to choose, the right to be informed, and the right to be heard.

In his thousand days as President, Kennedy generated a mood of discontent. Others seized on individual ills and by their words or actions began to shape the revolution. Rachel Carson's impassioned assault on the indiscriminate use of pesticides and herbicides spelled out the problems, and also identified the culprit. "This is an era of specialists," she wrote in *Silent Spring,** "each of whom sees his own problem and is unaware of or intolerant of the larger frame into which it fits. It is also an era dominated by industry, in which the right to make a dollar at whatever cost is seldom challenged. When the public protests, confronted with some obvious evidence of damaging results of pesticide applications it is fed little tranquilizing pills of half truth. We urgently need an end to these false assurances, to the sugar coating of unpalatable facts." The chemical industry's response was to latch on to exaggerations in the book and conduct a frontal assault on its whole premise. A weak pesticide-control law was passed, but the industry's blind and vicious attack revealed just how wide the gulf was between the boardroom and the backyard.

The pattern of the pesticides fight has been repeated in the 1960s with disappointing frequency. Each time the scene opened with a well-documented suggestion that something was amiss in the marketplace or in the environment. What followed was a fanatical defense of the status quo. Every suggestion that industry was not being totally responsible to society was rejected amid cries of outrage and attacks on the critics that often crossed the bounds of ordinary decency. Public relations firms (one of the more ignoble of America's institutions), trade associations and business societies all mobilized in massive retaliation.

Opportunities for reasoned private discussion in search of the facts were ignored, and public discussions in the press and in congressional hearings were conducted in an atmosphere of ideological conflict rather than rational debate. Now and then, questions raised by critics were effectively quelled. But more

*Houghton Mifflin, Boston, Mass., 1962.

often, the results of the battle against change that industry chose
to wage so energetically were disastrous. Inestimable damage was
done to the image of some industries not by the attackers, but by
the defenders, as they displayed a blind unconcern for any save
their own viewpoints. Overzealous minions of tuned-out corporate leaders often succeeded in making their industry look worse
than it really was, horrifying even their superiors with their
excesses. The nation was educated in the process; if industry is
seeking the source of the consumer movement's strength, it need
not look far.

Consider the drug industry, which regularly works wonders
in the most medically advanced nation in history. When Senator
Estes Kefauver suggested that drug profits ranging into the
thousands of per cent were unjustified, and unfair to the
consumer who often could not afford the price, the industry's
overdeveloped instinct for self-preservation instantly rose to the
challenge. The three-year battle against drug safety might have
been successful, but for a particularly grievous mistake made by
one of the industry's members that was revealed in the eleventh
hour.

On June 8, 1962, a group gathered in the Senate Judiciary
Committee hearing room including representatives of Senators
James Eastland and Everett Dirksen, committee staff, industry
lobbyists, and lawyer Lloyd Cutler, representing the Pharmaceutical Manufacturers Association (and later to represent the
auto industry in the safety hearings). Senator Kefauver had not
been invited to witness the emasculation of his bill. Thirteen
strong amendments were dropped, thirteen new ones were added,
most of them written by industry representatives, and the main
body of the bill was almost totally rewritten. As one staffer
lamely put it later: "The drug industry got more than we got."
The bill would have passed in its gutted form, but one month
later, one of the consumer's major weapons, Morton Mintz of *The
Washington Post*, wrote a story. Two years before, Mintz
reported, the William Merrell Company had begun its campaign to
market a tranquilizer containing the drug thalidomide. Its
application to the Food and Drug Administration was handled by
Dr. Frances Kelsey, a Canadian-born, 48-year-old doctor with
endless patience for detail. The drug had been tested on
laboratory animals, and was already on the market in Germany,

but Dr. Kelsey noted that animals and people reacted differently to the drug. For one thing, the drug failed to make animals sleepy. With the relevancy of the lab tests to humans thus thrown into question, Dr. Kelsey held up permission to market the drug. Merrell operatives, presumably concerned for their competitive position in the marketplace and anxious to move with a potential big seller, contacted Dr. Kelsey 50 separate times, and engaged in some personal conversations with other FDA officials regarding Dr. Kelsey that can only be classified as scurrilous. Even after the FDA notified Merrell that some severe and disabling cases of neuritis were occurring among thalidomide users in Europe, the pressure continued unabated. Then, after two years of steady heat, Merrell suddenly withdrew its application in the spring of 1962. Evidence had come through, Mintz reported, that thalidomide users were giving birth to tragically deformed babies.

The timing of the revelation was exquisite. The horrifying details of babies without limbs stilled the lobbyists, brought the most diffident of Congressmen to his feet in righteous indignation, and put the drug bill back into its original tough form which passed unanimously. The drug industry had spent millions of dollars in a systematic campaign to deprive the consumer of added protection, lowered costs, and increased knowledge. It earned for itself the enmity of millions of Americans who still remember that one woman doctor was all that stood between them and the most poignant of human tragedies.

The thalidomide case revealed to the nation how a company, in its haste to succeed, could fail to heed the red flags of warning. The battle over highway safety revealed the same tragic failing; the 53,000 yearly deaths on the highways were fully publicized and yet almost totally ignored by government, industry and consumer alike. When challenged to design a car that would be more forgiving of a driver's human fallibilities, the auto industry responded with the same blind obstinacy, and a similar personal attack was mounted on the principal critic. In this case, the target was Ralph Nader, who had concentrated on the engineering weaknesses of the General Motors Corvair in his book, *Unsafe at Any Speed*.* In the middle of the auto safety hearings, orders went out from GM in Detroit to "get something" on Nader. Private detective Vincent Gillen attempted to determine that Nader liked girls, or that alternatively he didn't like girls, or that he had some other personal weakness that presumably would show his incompetency to speak out against needless death on the highway. Nader, who turned out to be distressingly normal and acutely able to defend himself, was nevertheless shaken by the sordid episode. And when the nation read how its greatest and largest corporation had felt threatened enough by a single individual to attempt to destroy him both professionally and personally, the battle was suddenly over. One Senator spoke eloquently for all his colleagues when he said: "The hell with them." The bill passed. Where four million yearly auto injuries had failed to disturb a nation, one attempt at character assassination put a dent in the chromework that still dulls the industry's image.

The self-defeating exercises practiced by the drug and auto industries has been repeated time and again by many of the major industries of the United States. It is often the industry's own actions—or its religious devotion to the cause of inaction—that gets bills passed. The more perceptive advisers to the American marketplace have warned that industry's style in handling the complaints of the consumerists is a mistake, but the message sinks in very slowly. *Advertising Age* columnist Stanley Cohen recently spelled out this massive misjudgment: "The worst disasters for business occur when executives and Washington lobbyists assume that, right or wrong, they can stand pat and mobilize enough political power to have their way. When things go wrong—as they did for the drug industry when the thalidomide scandal broke in 1962, and the auto industry when auto safety legislation was pending—congressional support silently slips away. When the industry is caught with its hands in the cookie jar. . .millions of dollars in customer good will goes down the drain. . . . When they complain about the rise of consumer power, business executives should consider who has been creating the opportunities. Nobody ever heard of Ralph Nader until General Motors put a detective on his trail."

But the attitude remains: consumerism is a temporary aberration, currently threatening the American way of business with its cheap play to the emotions. Some call it "consumeritis," which Edward Thiele, president of the Leo Burnett advertising firm, diagnosed as "...a contagious inflammation of the consumer-interest portion of the brain often resulting from political ambition or desire to derive favor from groups of consumers through personal publicity. Symptoms include a strong tendency to invent issues where no real issues exist. If not treated, severe cases may lead to demagoguery." His comments came in a speech to the National Association of Food Chains. The association went on from there to join in the attack against the meat-inspection bill. It was the consumerists' opinion that meat manufactured and sold within a state, and therefore not subject to Federal inspection, was often adulterated, deceiving the consumer if not endangering him. When the Agriculture Department visited Safeway, A&P, Kroger, and First National stores in 28 states and purchased 162 samples of locally-produced frank-furters, ground beef and other processed meat, it found 123 of them adulterated and below Federal standards. Yet the thesis that no real issues exist is still heard.

The list of legislative victories scored so far in the 1960s indicates otherwise: unsafe and ineffective drugs, deceptive packaging and labeling, unsafe cars, flammable fabrics, substand-ard tires, impure meat, fish and poultry, unsafe gas pipelines, unfair credit practices, misleading product warranties, excessive radiation, polluted water and air. Some of the laws that have passed are weak and ineffective: Nader good-naturedly calls the deceptive packaging law of 1966 "the most deceptive package of all." But most are real laws, with substantial enforcement provisions. And as each battle was fought and won, the structural underpinnings for the next battle grew stronger.

It has become increasingly clear to all but the most hopelessly committed anticonsumerists that the problems are real, and soluble without disrupting the economy. General Motors' installation of collapsible steering columns in its autos (after it became clear they would soon be required by Federal law) has amply demonstrated that dramatic steps toward safety could be made by the industry if it chose to. Accident statistics indicate a dramatic drop in deaths inflicted by the steering column; officials of the Federal Highway Administration believe that the ultimate savings will be 10,000 lives annually. According to the testimony of The University of Michigan Highway Safety Research Institute, the engineering job on compressible steering columns was letter-perfect—the institute suggested that the government should not interfere.

Technological advances such as this one have occurred, however, only after a change in attitude had liberated talents long suppressed. And the change in attitude came about only after sustained and effective effort had forced the change. It is this strength to sustain its drive that has set the consumer movement of the 1960s apart from earlier ones, a strength that is composed of four human elements.

First, the reformers who identify and publicize these issues are a far cry from the muckrakers of the past. Men such as Nader, and some congressional committee staffers, are not reformers. They are lawyers representing the traditionally unrepresented side of the buyer-seller relationship. They do their homework very carefully, rarely make mistakes, and pursue an issue to completion. They work through the legislative process, not against it, and attack an industry's shortcomings, not industry itself. There is no consumer advocate of today whose target is capitalism, or whose ideology is communism. The battle is not ideological at all; it is practical. Reformers of the past were mostly bomb-throwers, unyielding enemies of the American business system, or idle dreamers pursuing an unattainable Utopia. The new breed of consumer advocate, as he is more properly called, is a hard-nosed practitioner of the art of the possible, and usually offers remedies that are constructive, and do no violence to industry. Any consumer advocate would willingly return to the doctrine of *caveat emptor* if its essential ingredient could be restored—buyer and seller on equal terms.

Second, journalists have accurately and effectively picked up the causes espoused by consumer advocates. Journalism, whether in books, periodicals, or daily papers, has played a key role in each of the three major consumer movements. But its role in the 1960s is less impassioned and more reasoned than in the past. Some, such as Fred Zimmerman of *The Wall Street Journal* and Stanley Cohen of *Ad Age*, operate from bases that exist primarily for the edification of businessmen. Others have become experts, such as *The Washington Post's* Morton Mintz, an authority on the drug industry. Their efforts are recognized as legitimate exercises of the journalistic art: Nick Kotz of *Cowles Publications* won a Pulitzer Prize for his pieces on the meat-inspection fight. Publishers recognize their reporters' stories as bona fide news, and pressure to "tone down" a story is minimal.

Third, politicians are now actively aiding the cause of the consumer, and often leading it. In Congress, legislators have discovered that the political danger of opposing industry and espousing consumer causes has been greatly exaggerated. Consumer causes win some votes and lose some. One leading senator's home-state polls show that his activities in the field play a minor role in making up his constituents' minds. The issue is politically neutral enough for legislators to exercise their own feelings without risking their careers. Thus many legislators are taking advantage of the rare opportunity to act purely on principle. Missouri Democrat Leonor Sullivan waged a six-month battle for the truth-in-lending bill that primarily aided the Eastern big-city ghetto resident. Others run directly against special interests in their state: Minnesota's Senator Walter F. Mondale played a key role in getting a strong meat-inspection bill passed, and Senator Edmund Muskie led the water-pollution fight from his base in heavily polluted Maine.

Fourth, two presidents have institutionalized the consumer movement in the government. The Consumer Advisory Council created by President Kennedy later evolved into the office of the Special Assistant for Consumer Affairs. Under President Johnson, the office has given the government a focal point which attracts 500 to 600 pieces of mail a week and responds with a fairly steady barrage of speechmaking on the cutting edge of the movement. The first official suggestion that home appliances should reveal their design lifetime to prospective buyers came from Betty Furness. When the truth-in-lending bill appeared in danger of being watered down, a hurry-up news conference was called to expose the latest wrinkles in credit practices. The President chose Miss Furness to go around his hidebound Agriculture Department and put his full support behind the tough version of the meat bill. The office, now running with a complement of 24 people, is a permanent institution, in little danger of being closed up by a future administration no matter how the political winds blow. The office is known to the public, and the political costs of abolishing it would be high.

The combined pressure of these four elements has generated a body of legislation which has become the structural framework for the movement. How that framework is filled out depends heavily on budgetary limitations. It also depends on how well Congress does its job of following up the laws of the land with spot investigations and oversight hearings, which is not Congress' strong suit. But however well pursued the spirit of the laws are, the letter of the laws represent in general an attempt to enforce a sense of social responsibility on the inhabitants of the marketplace.

Some in the community do a disservice by suggesting that democracy is threatened by such legislation. In a talk to an American Advertising Federation conference, Arthur C. Fatt of Grey Advertising said that he was "concerned that if the government continues its policy of portraying the business community in the worst possible light that it will severely damage our economic and social structure. . . ." His dire concern was nowhere documented, as it cannot be. But the entire speech intoned darkly of the threat to The American Way, suggesting at one point that government tampering with the marketplace will deprive the consumer of his rights to make his own choice in the marketplace. As an example of what happens to a people under the paternalistic hand of Big Brother, Mr. Fatt points to the American Indian.

This type of attack on government's role in the marketplace has worked fairly well for more than 50 years. It was used in 1914 to oppose the Federal Trade Commission, an understaffed institution which Mr. Fatt praises as a "fine instrument." Fortunately, however, such sentiments are little heeded anymore, and there are progressively fewer residents of the business community who use this tactic in an attempt to scare off government officials. More and more, businessmen with a more modern approach, or at least with a more realistic one, recognize that things could be better. Robert L. Wells, an officer of Westinghouse, told his colleagues at a mid-western convention in 1968: "We must realize that the public is staging a 'revolt of rising expectancy.' Customers today expect products to perform satisfactorily, to provide dependable functional performance and to be safe. This threshold of acceptable performance is steadily rising. . . ."

None of the expectations that Mr. Wells lists seems outlandish; the amazing thing is that it took until 1968 for it to be said. His statement recognizes that the consumer's expectations were quite successfully suppressed for many years. If there has been paternalism exercised by any segment of the American society, it has been exercised by business. Advertising's primary role, for example, is to shape consumer choices by repetition of a product name, not by delivering information. The proof is in advertising expenditure figures. Unique products such as *Corfam* shoes are given a big sendoff concentrating on the unique quality of the product, then taper off. But closely interchangeable or identical products such as toothpaste must advertise constantly and heavily because they have no unique quality beyond any other product on the market. When a product that is significantly better comes along, such as *Crest* and the later fluoridated toothpastes, it must be advertised incessantly in order to be heard through the din, and the standard products, now made obsolete by science, must redouble their efforts to keep from being out-sold by a superior product. This paternalistic attempt to make up the consumer's mind for him continues to the supermarket shelf, where the consumer's ability to make a meaningful choice on basis of price is systematically blunted by deceptive packaging techniques. Toothpastes exist in 57 different sizes on the shelf. With weights broken down into tenths of an ounce, and prices broken down into hundredths of the dollar, it is utterly impossible to determine which tube is the most economical buy without pencil, paper, and a considerable investment of time. If anybody is making the consumer's decisions for him, it is business, not government.

The same sort of paternalism is practiced throughout industry. Autos are traditionally sold on the basis of styling, which is irrelevant to the purpose of the car. Evidence that the consumer is not quite so mesmerized by sleek lines is accumulating, though. Heavy sales of imports such as the *Volkswagen* have been aided by ad campaigns that push practicality and downgrade style. *Dodge Darts* are making inroads in the market because the car has a good performance record and low price, while other makers of compacts grumble that this shouldn't happen because the *Dart* has a dull and conservative style.

The fight to place the consumer on equal terms with the
seller has been raging for most of this decade, and there are
some signs that the business community is beginning to understand what the fight is all about. It is not aimed at wrapping
business in chains but rather freeing business from the
shackles it has placed on itself. The object is to elicit a more
responsive and responsible level of performance from industry,
and not to impose one—though it will be imposed by legislation if
the necessary evolution in attitude does not take place. With
increasing frequency, this is exactly the advice that the business
community is giving itself. An influential newsletter advised its
clients in 1968 that businessmen had better do more self-policing
to get at practices that have raised consumer hackles. "It's partly
to fend off consumer laws. . .But mostly it's in response to public
pressure, a near-revolt against false and misleading ads, bait-
selling, poor product performance, inadequate service, fuzzy
warranties, policies on returning goods, etc. . . . Some businessmen object to all this, figure that most consumers can take care
of themselves. But others say that unless business acts now it
faces more government regulation. And no businessman is in
favor of that."

The alternative to punitive and preventive legislation is for
industry to drop its automatic resistance to change. It is
beginning to happen. In the spring of 1968, General Motors
announced that it would install side guard rails in most of its
1969 models, to make occupants less vulnerable to side impacts.
A few weeks later, Ford promised that its more expensive lines
would offer a computerized anti-skid device in 1969, which will
prevent wheels from locking during an emergency stop. Ford also
revealed that the front end of its lower-priced models would be
altered to soak up more of the shock of a collision before it
reaches the driver.

Three years before, the auto industry was steadfastly
absolving itself of all responsibility for the nation's toll of death
on the highway. Suddenly, it had begun competing to build a
safer car, in advance of any new standards set by the Federal
Highway Administration.

The individual consumer cannot effect these changes by
himself. As the housewives' boycott against the supermarkets
revealed a few years ago, even collective action with heavy press

coverage does no more than create a minor and temporary public-relations problem for the chain store. Sooner or later, the consumer has to return to the storeshelf, for he has to consume, making his choices as best he can in the world's largest, most abundant—and most confusing—marketplace. "The fact is," Ralph Nader once observed to a Senate hearing, "it is not an equal contest."

In a speech to the National Association of Manufacturers, then Under Secretary of Commerce Howard Samuels asserted: "The consumer is faced with a bewildering variety of goods and complexity of products. He has no way of determining for himself whether one tape recorder is better made than another. He does not have time to 'comparison shop' between prices and contents of 8,000 different items in the supermarket. So he is impatient with producers and marketers of those goods when he finds something that does not meet the standards he expected. And he is better educated. He is not willing to suffer in silence." His impatience is more often converted into the only sort of action he can take—a letter to the manufacturer or to the government, the only two organs of society which can effect meaningful changes.

The choice, says Bronson LaFollette, Attorney General for the State of Wisconsin and chairman of the President's Consumer Advisory Council, is clear: continued warfare between business and government, or cooperation and interaction between the two forces. "It seems to me," LaFollette told the same NAM meeting, "that interaction is the key to developing the kind of consumer protection programs that everyone can live with. I'm sure that industry would rather play a role in developing a program it can live with rather than being dragged, kicking and yelping, and finally having it stuffed down its throat."

Responsiveness to the demands of society will do far more to preserve a free-enterprise economy than religious opposition to change. Said LaFollette: "The important thing for the critics of present day consumer legislation to realize is such legislation is not aimed in any dramatic new direction—that it is simply directed at making our private enterprise economy function more efficiently. Such proposed legislation is well within the tradition of what the National Association of Manufacturers likes to call 'the American individual enterprise system,' with its 'dependency on free individuals, responsible for results of their own decisions'."

Freedom in the marketplace is everyone's goal—business, government, and the consumer. But freedom in the marketplace is also becoming the goal for everyone in it, to be achieved, as Senator Warren Magnuson says, by exorcizing "the ghost of *caveat emptor*, which pits buyer against seller in a malevolent relationship."

Much has been done to exorcise that ghost. But many areas remain that have received only scant attention, or ineffective legislation. In the next few years, new ground will be broken, and old battlegrounds revisited. The main pressure for change will come from the government, but some changes will be made by industry itself. Some of the biggest trouble spots:

Cigarettes: In Washington, the agony of forming a public policy on cigarette smoking is just beginning. Smoking is not strictly a consumer issue because the smoker surely knows by now that cigarettes are harmful. It is, instead, a public health issue, one that is about to be faced head-on by Congress, five years after the Surgeon General's report linked cigarettes to lung cancer.

The most recent reports have served to confirm the earlier judgments, and added significant information connecting smoking with bronchitis, emphysema, and coronary heart disease. The 1968 report showed new evidence that the first heart attack is much more likely to be fatal if the victim is a smoker. It also showed that lung cancer in women is on the rise, weakening industry's defense that lung cancer was a quirk in the male makeup. "The magnitude of the health problem from smoking is enormous," says Senator Magnuson.

But the magnitude of the political and economic problems of smoking is just as large. In a surprise ruling, the Federal Trade Commission voted three to two in 1968 to ban all cigarette advertising from radio and TV. Under voluntary strictures to control the timing and amount of advertising, the industry's expenditures for TV spots increased to $230 million in 1967 from the 1964 level of $170 million. Per capita consumption of cigarettes has dropped since the cancer threat first became known, but still, nearly 600 billion cigarettes were manufactured in the United States in 1967.

There is little chance that Congress will endorse the FTC's ban on advertising, nor does the FTC really expect an endorsement. The drastic suggestion was primarily a device to stir up some action that will be effective. Before 1969 is over, it is likely that new regulations will be placed on commercials, limiting their use to times when the children are in bed. But as long as tobacco is such a big cash crop for the South Atlantic states, neither cigarettes nor their advertising will be banned. The best course for the consumerists is to press for development of new, more benign strains of tobacco, and more effective filtration. There has been some progress in the latter, but the former has been hardly explored, and could have more profound results.

Life Insurance: After a period of rapid expansion and high sales after the war, the insurance industry is in trouble. The boom years are past, and the industry is overcrowded with marginally competent and unnecessary companies. Between 500 and 600 companies, analysts estimate, will disappear in the next few years. Hopefully, they will disappear through mergers, and not by failures that leave their customers defenseless.

Many of the smaller companies cannot support themselves by sales of policies. Their survival depends on how wisely they invest their capital in other ventures. In effect, therefore, life insurance is just a sideline for many companies, and in fact many company directors have been accused of treating insurance sales as merely a device to generate income for their other interests. The situation is so delicate that many state regulatory agencies have been quietly advising borderline companies to merge before it is too late.

The consumer's problems have also grown steadily. The need to keep sales volume high has led to a confusing whirl of insurance plans, packages, and sales pitches. Probes by mail and telephone are constant, and once inside the door, the salesman is more than ever tempted to deceive or mislead in order to make the sale.

Some states have effective laws and agencies to control the industry, but many don't. And for the larger companies, the problems of dealing with a hodgepodge of 50 different sets of laws has generated some desire within the industry for uniform, countrywide guidelines set by Washington.

The auto insurance industry is already the subject of a two-year Federal study. The same course is likely for the life-insurance industry. Tangible results that would help the consumer are years away, however, because the industry and the issues are so large and intricate. Meanwhile, the best course is to read *Consumer Reports'* book on the subject.

Credit Ratings: Whether he knows it or not, the consumer's ability to buy on the installment plan is not up to him. The privilege is proffered by a credit-rating service. All manner of information—relevant and irrelevant, correct and incorrect, fair and unfair—is collected by these agencies from banks, stores, and other past creditors, processed according to the agencies' own guidelines, and then issued to any subscriber on request. A bad rating is final and unassailable.

Concern has been growing for the civil rights of private citizens who find themselves involuntarily labeled. They have no say on their rating, no access to the information filed on them, no means of confronting their accusers, defending themselves, or setting the record straight. And in many cases, the information gets into the wrong hands, including the hands of some government law-enforcement agencies.

Senator William Proxmire, who helped lead the fight for the truth-in-lending bill, hopes to correct the flaws in the credit-rating business. A bill he has prepared is designed to provide some safeguards for the buying public.

"My bill would require three things," he said in announcing his intention to press for legislation. "It would require, first, that credit bureaus have in effect procedures for guaranteeing the confidentiality of the information they collect and that no such information be released to noncreditors such as governmental investigatory agencies without the express consent of the person involved.

"The bill would require, second, that an individual be given an opportunity to correct adverse information in his credit record at his request and that he be notified when a derogatory item of public record is entered in his credit record.

"And, third, the bill would require that there be procedures for discarding irrelevant and out-dated information in an individual's credit file."

Credit-rating bureaus are necessary, because some consumers overextend themselves, and some others, perhaps taking their morals from the marketplace, think that a department store is fair game for their calculated irresponsibility. But they are currently almost totally unregulated, and Federal guidelines seem a sure thing.

Services and Repairs: The frustrations of finding a good, honest repairman are not the consumer's alone. Industry can't find them, either, and the government doesn't quite know what to do about it. It is not even clear to anyone yet whether the government should get involved at all. But the pressures on Washington from the nation's consumers are practically irresistible. A steady stream of letters pours into Congress and the White House pleading with officials to do something, anything. Industry's response to the problem has been to establish training schools for servicemen, but poor quality control on products leaving the assembly line generates more work than the added talent in the field can handle.

What happens depends on how well government and industry cooperate in finding a solution. There is very little the government can do alone, except to provide incentives through the job-training programs, and to give the once honored role of Mr. Fixit new status and visibility. Without industry help, however, the government is likely to be compelled to try something. Some officials are already weighing a scheme to license repairmen as a means of raising their quality and insuring their honesty. But setting higher standards would reduce the already short supply of servicemen, and any licensing procedure contains the danger of corruption. Any attempt by the government to legislate reliable and honest servicemen into existence might create more problems than solutions. But government action can easily be warded off by the private sector, and the government is willing to wait for suggestions, for a while.

Voluntary Standards: Many industries, including those involved in producing electrical and power equipment, adhere to standards set by industry itself. Underwriter's Laboratories is one example. But the alarming rate of home accidents, and the questionable safety of many "approved" products led President Johnson in 1968 to create a task force on product safety. One of the subjects being studied by the task force is the adequacy of industry's voluntary standards. Some 200 products in common use around the home are also being studied, and if those under voluntary standards do not measure up, Washington will move to bolster or supplant industry's guidelines with new, stiffer ones of its own—backed by civil or criminal penalties.

Advertising: The $17-billion advertising industry has been waiting for years for the Federal bombs to start falling. But there is no new attack coming. Government officials lack both the appetite and the inclination to try working any major change in the industry. They also view advertising as merely one expression of the real problem, the madly confused marketing system.

But since advertising is the most visible and audible part of that system, pressure from both the Federal Trade Commission and from private consumer advocates will be constant. The industry's own excesses, visible to the consumer every day, plus the bad publicity that follows these excesses, is affecting the industry's sole reason for existing—its ability to sell. Pressure is also increasing for the industry to put its talents to constructive uses, by adding a healthy dose of public service to its sales pitches. The industry's problems have started internal rumblings to raise standards of performance. Hard-sell hucksters ("fast, fast, FAST relief") are out of favor with their colleagues, though they are proving remarkably resistant to social pressures.

Only if the industry fails to evolve will there be Federal action. European styles of limiting ad agencies are well-known to American officials; many types of claims, such as ones of comparative superiority and mention of other brand names, are flatly ruled out. The Federal Trade Commission's powers over unfair and deceptive trade practices, and the Federal Communications Commission's control over the airwaves are powerful weapons, when used. The first moves, however, will come from the industry. "We have got to become more relevant," is the way the chairman of one large ad agency put it. Relevancy has always been the industry's problem.

Dr. Wiley's Rebellion

chapter 2

The United States in the nineteenth century compiled a record of growth in size, wealth, and power unparalleled in history. From Jefferson to McKinley, the government did all it could to foster the move westward, aid the rise of industry, and increase its standing in the world. By 1900, the country had grown from 16 to 45 states, increased its yearly output of goods and services to $19 billion. It began the century under constant threat from the imperialistic powers of Europe, and ended it preaching the need to expand into backward areas and with a victory against Spain in its first two-ocean war.

The mood of the times didn't permit the government to stop and consider how the relationship of its people to this growing giant was evolving. The American citizen was part of the nation's wealth and power, contributing to the common good with his labor, making his own way uniquely free of government interference—and uniquely free of government protection from the commercial and industrial juggernaut growing up around him.

Protection, or regulation, was not even an issue. Government activities in the American economy were designed to provide fertile ground for growth and no more. In a primarily agricultural economy, there was little else to do; the Jeffersonian ideal of a simple agrarian society seemed to serve the nation and its people well enough. When some industry began to spring up after the War of 1812, a touch of Alexander Hamilton's economics was added in the form of a protective tariff to control foreign competition. By the time of the Civil War, only a million people were earning their livings in manufacturing, and the total output of manufactured goods in the U.S. was $2 billion. Forty years later, at the turn of the century, those figures had rocketed to five million employees generating $11 billion worth of goods.

The change from agriculture to industry was rapid and profound. But the nation's philosophy failed to change with it. The hands-off doctrine of *laissez-faire* continued to dominate, along with a Protestant Ethic that praised hard work, treated poverty as a crime and wealth as a social virtue. The fittest survived, and the weak suffered with their own deficiencies. It was the "natural law" of economics. "Industrial success can be won at a price," an economist of the day wrote, "and the price is observance of the inevitable rules of the game—namely, sobriety, industry, saving, avoidance of speculation, knowledge of human nature, good judgment, common sense, persistence, intelligence, and integrity. No social system ever keeps men down who have these qualities." A man possessed of all those virtues would make out fairly well in the world, but the ethic was rather harsh judgment on the great bulk of America's citizens not so well endowed.

Government "paternalism" was heresy, sure to destroy the qualities of rugged individualism, the spirit of self-reliance, the sense of personal responsibility, and the other ennobling virtues which presumably were possessed by the children of the wealthy and the poor, the privileged and the exploited alike. A government official put it bluntly: "Once let the idea go forth that it is the duty of the state to take care of everybody, and everybody will cease to take care of himself." Thus it was more than an expedient philosophy. It was, to the influentials of the day, the foundationstone of society, the credo of freedom preached both from the pulpit and the corporate office, and sincerely meant. For the consumer, *caveat emptor* was more than a warning; it was a proper doctrine to be cherished by the purchaser of industry's wares as the rightful expression of his individualism. Some of the more naive exponents of this philosophy believed the consumer perfectly capable of defending himself against any possible wrongdoing by industry. A powerful Congressman of the 1880's, Maine's Thomas Reed, thought the growing concern over monopoly and trusts ridiculous. "What unreasonable talk this is," he temporized. "A dozen men fix the price for sixty million freemen! They can never do it! There is no power on earth that can raise the price of any necessity of life above a just price and keep it there. More than that, if the price is raised and maintained even for a short while, it means ruin for the combination and still lower prices for the consumers." Mr. Reed honestly believed that the consumer was king. But the consumer was in reality a pawn and the Big Businessmen of the day knew it, relied on it, and were occasionally even honest enough to admit it. Henry O. Havemeyer, president of the Sugar Trust which was then controlling the entire industry (final price included despite Mr. Reed's abiding faith), put it succinctly: "Let the buyer beware; that covers the whole business. You can not wet nurse people from the time they are born until the time they die. They have got to wade in and get stuck, and that is the way men are educated and cultivated." Small wonder then, that in this climate only one major piece of consumer-protection legislation became law in all of the 19th Century. The Mail Fraud Act of 1872 helped slow down the abuses in one corner of the marketplace.

By mid-century, legions of rugged individualists had developed a surpassing skill at the art of the con and the swindle. At first it was man against man; the shell game and the confidence scheme practiced by an itinerant pitchman who departed the scene before the sucker realized he was being taken. But with the growth of the U.S. Postal Service, the more enterprising swindlers soon realized they could expand their operations dramatically, and also avoid face-to-face dealings that occasionally ended looking down the barrel of a shotgun.

Mail fraud was simple, involving almost no risk. Operating in one state from a safe haven in another, the swindler was almost immune from the law. The Federal government had no jurisdiction to step into a city or state to halt the offender, and any man who was taken by the lure of a quick fortune had to suffer his empty pockets and shattered ego alone.

But ultimately, so many constituents wrote angry or pleading letters to their Congressmen, and the mails acquired such an unhealthy reputation of being in league with crooks (many a postal clerk participated in a scheme or concocted one of his own) that pressures built in Washington for action. Once the desire to do something had grown strong enough, the solution was obvious: though the Federal Government could do little to outlaw the schemes themselves except by an endless series of laws against every new trick, the use of the Federally-run mails to carry out fraudulent operations could indeed be ruled out. The result was the Mail Fraud Act.

The law subjected anyone to penalties for "having devised or intending to devise any scheme or artifice to defraud," and then using the mails to carry out the scheme. It was not necessary for the con man to succeed in his game. If an innocent-looking piece of mail offering a charming European bride at a reasonable price or a fistful of mining stock that could lead to a fortune had a fraudulent intent behind it, that was enough to earn the offender a $500 fine and as much as eighteen months in jail. Mere intent—a word that has continually generated debate through the history of consumer legislation—was inherently unfair, and illegal. The law was tough, and the courts enforced it with great vigor, taking the phrase "any scheme or artifice to defraud" at its widest possible meaning. Blackmail and extortion, con games, inheritance schemes, stock swindles and marriage schemes fell easily before the prosecutors' attacks.

The courts stopped short only when a scheme involved just the individuals on either end of a letter. In one such case, a certain Mr. Owens, in debt to his supplier of whiskey for $162.50, mailed his creditor a fifty-cent piece and a sheaf of blank, dollar-size paper. His apparent hope that the distiller's bookkeeper might not notice landed him in court, charged with violation of the Mail Fraud Act. The court dismissed the case. Expressing no desire to get involved in every piece of correspondence between individuals, the court set the following precedent: "It appears to the court that the act was designated to strike at common schemes of fraud, whereby through the post office, circulars etc., are distributed, generally to entrap and defraud the unwary." Mr. Owens' bill still had to be paid, but he was guilty of no Federal crime.

The law was strengthened in 1889 with the passage of amendments to cover the sale of worthless articles, known in the trade as "green articles," "green coin," "paper goods," and a host of other names, all of which were included in the language of the law to be sure that everyone knew exactly what was covered. Seven years later, the key ingredient to the statute was tested in the Supreme Court (Durland vs. United States), and the landmark case firmly established the doctrine that intent to defraud was crime enough. The case involved the sale of securities. The price of the securities was clearly stated, and the terms under which a fortune would come the purchaser's way were contained right in the wording on the securities. But the seller had utterly no intention of trying to deliver anything beyond the worthless piece of paper. He made no promises. He lured his victims only with the possibility of profit.

The defense steadfastly contended that the indictment "discloses on its face absolutely nothing but an intention to commit a violation of a contract. If there is one principle of criminal law that is absolutely settled by an overwhelming avalanche of authority it is that fraud. . .must be the misrepresentation of an existing or a past fact, and cannot consist of the mere intention not to carry out a contract in the future."

The court disagreed most emphatically. "If the testimony," the court ruled, "had shown that this. . .company, and the defendant, as its president, had entered in good faith upon that business, believing that out of the moneys received they could by investment or otherwise make enough to justify the promised returns, no conviction could be sustained, no matter how visionary might seem the scheme. The charge is that in putting forth this scheme it was not the intent of the defendant to make an honest effort for its success, but that he resorted to this form and pretense of a bond without a thought that he or the company would ever make good its promises. It was with the purpose of protecting the public against all such intentional efforts to despoil, and to prevent the post office from being used to carry them into effect, that this statute was passed; and it would strip it of value to confine it to such cases as disclosed an actual misrepresentation as to some existing fact, and exclude those in which is only the allurement of a specious and glittering promise."

The "specious and glittering promise" still arrives in the mails today. The mail fraud statute, often amended to keep up with the endless imaginations of the swindlers, now makes it illegal to defraud, or to obtain money or property "by means of false or fraudulent pretense, representations, or promises," or to "sell, dispose of, loan, exchange, alter, give away, distribute, supply or furnish or procure" anything that is counterfeit or spurious. Even the most ingenious of con men would be hard put to find loopholes in the law. He relies instead on the law moving slower than he does, and counts on his victim's embarrassed silence instead of a more appropriate response, a phone call to the authorities.

It was inevitable that outright attempts to defraud the public would sooner or later lead to strong governmental action. A con man whose sole purpose in life is to cheat his neighbor can find little redeeming social purpose to his actions when hauled into court. He is a fly-by-night operator, with no name, no status, no lobby. But other "schemes or artifices" abounded in the nation at the same period, less apparent and sometimes totally unnoticed, less malevolent in their purpose, but infinitely more dangerous. The danger and deception that grew along with the rise in food-processing, and in the blossoming of the patent-medicine business, threatened the health of a nation.

The rapid growth of transportation in the United States after the Civil War opened new markets for food producers, and made the old markets more readily accessible from greater distances. As the people became more mobile, so did their products; New Yorkers ate canned meat from Chicago, the Chicagoans enjoyed canned peas from Eastern farms. But the new techniques in food-preserving were still imperfect, and certain steps were taken by industry to assure that the food was still edible—or at least apparently so—when it reached the table. With the science of chemistry far more advanced than biology, particularly bacteriology, more benign forms of preservation such as aseptic canneries and careful sterilization were rarely practiced. The general practice was to give the foodstuff a stiff dose of medicine so that it wouldn't come down with something on the way to the grocery shelf.

Formaldehyde—embalming fluid—was a favorite preservative for meat. Peas and other green vegetables, which lost their farm-fresh color during processing, were given a dose of copper sulphate, an appropriately green but highly toxic chemical, to restore "freshness." Wherever needed, artificial coloring or artificial flavoring were added to restore produce to the appearance and taste it originally possessed.

The morality of amorality of such steps was hardly an issue to the food-processors. The doses of chemicals in food were not high enough to make anybody acutely ill—not often enough, at least, to attract any attention. Long-term effects of coal-tar dyes, since identified as cancer-causing agents, were not discovered for decades. Kidney trouble was passed off as one of the risks of living; no one sensed that the job of purging the daily doses of preservatives might be overtaxing the organs. If any thought that formaldehyde was not a proper substance for ingestion passed through the minds of the producers, it moved on very rapidly, for the preservative was a necessity. The system made it necessary. A producer operating in a competitive profit system could not risk the loss of a carload of meat due to spoilage, or rejection in the marketplace of an off-color pea. His prime goal was survival of the operation, financial success its measure of social virtue. A cannery-owner was responsible for the livelihood of dozens or hundreds of employees, and responsible to his own ethic that the worst crime against society was to fail.

It is impossible to establish a cause-and-effect relationship, but it is at least interesting to note that the rise of questionably preserved foodstuffs paralleled the tremendous growth in sales of nostrums at the corner drugstore. One way or another, the patent medicines of the day changed the internal state of the self-healer. Hostetter's Stomach Bitters certainly improved the mood after a spoonful or two—it contained 44.3 per cent alcohol. More insidious was the indiscriminate use of narcotics in unlabeled compounds, sold to cure everything from headaches to cancer.

In all the Federal Government, there was only one institution that by its charter could have taken systematic interest in the question of pure food and drugs. The Agriculture Department had been created in 1862 by Abraham Lincoln to be "the people's department." But for two decades, the department had little time or inclination to be the people's department. Its major act in consumer protection was to question the adulteration of fertilizers and feedstuffs, which robbed the farmer of fair value for his money, and cheated the hogs out of a square meal. It was not until 1883 that the department embarked on a program of investigation and agitation to protect the consumer, and for two more decades it was virtually a one-man crusade.

The crusader was Dr. Harvey W. Wiley. Born on a backwoods Indiana farm, he had only scant education until he walked off to Hanover College five miles down the road at the age of eighteen. It took him more than a year to bring himself up to the level where he qualified as a freshman. But from there he went on to earn a medical degree from Indiana Medical College, and a science degree from Harvard, specializing in the analytical side of chemistry. A professorship at Purdue followed, where he became an internationally-known authority on sugar chemistry—particularly on glucose, a cheap sugar made from corn and used as an adulterant to cut costs of the more expensive syrups made from cane or maple sap. His efforts to create a domestic sugar industry caught the attention of Washington, where by coincidence the head of the Chemistry division in the Department of Agriculture had been fired over the same question. Wiley was given the job. Though his name is over shadowed by those of some of the muckrakers who were to come along later, Dr. Wiley is properly the hero of the Pure Food and Drug Act that passed 23 years later.

The long struggle to get some legislation passed is in many ways remarkably similar to other battles for the consumer still being fought. Wiley's chief obstacles were ignorance, indifference, and industry. They were also his chief allies: the massive ignorance that surrounded food adulteration and contamination made it relatively easy for him to become the leading authority on the subject; the continuing indifference of the citizenry and Wiley's own superiors, sadly enough, permitted the situation to become so bad that the ultimate revulsion was strong enough to carry the bill through; and some sectors of industry were just as interested in having other sectors of industry brought under Federal control as Wiley was.

Wiley's first act was to set his staff to searching for questionable or dangerous ingredients in foods. They had little difficulty. Though they—and the consumer—had few labels to guide them, Wiley and his staff filled 1,400 pages of a ten-part department bulletin with documented cases of adulteration. They found everything from charcoal in pepper to sulphurous acid in canned vegetables, whiskey made of nothing but ethyl alcohol, flavoring, and coloring, and "potted chicken" composed entirely of beef and pork. But the reports were highly technical in nature, and had little effect on the public. An attempt by Wiley in 1890 to popularize the reports as a goad to action helped some. Laws passed Congress in 1890 and 1891 calling for inspection of animals for diseases, but these were primarily a result of embargoes and complaints from Europe on the quality of U.S. meat—namely, the threat of trichinosis. And no provisions for inspection of the animal as it was processed were included in the bills.

In the quarter-century before the food and drug bill finally passed Congress, more than 100 such acts were introduced. In some cases, industry supported the legislation. Dairy interests resented the incursions on the butter market being made by oleomargarine producers. Kentucky distilleries proud of their straight whiskey wanted the rubbing-alcohol variety labeled as "imitation whiskey" or some other such dispiriting phrase. But the result was usually a stalemate between lobbies. In 1892 a respectable food and drug law did manage to pass the Senate, but opposing interests kept it bottled up in a House committee until the session ended and the bill died. Another bill in 1897 met a similar fate.

Throughout these first unrewarding years, Wiley managed to maintain his objectivity—a prime requisite for a social reformer interested in succeeding rather than merely making noise. But he was beginning to learn that noise and notoriety helped his cause, even when it was somewhat misdirected. During the Spanish-American War, wild stories that bad beef was being fed to America's fighting men abounded in the press. Wiley conducted a thorough investigation, and found the reports to be "purely sensational and without foundation." But the outcome of the case failed to distract the public from what apparently was a novel thought—it was possible that the foods on the dinner table were not entirely wholesome. The background on Wiley and his long investigations that came out during the bad-beef investigation added to this growing queasiness in the public stomach. And when the public became more concerned, Congress became more responsive.

In 1902, Wiley finally won one fight. An amendment to that year's appropriation bill gave the department the right to establish standards of purity on food, and the characterize and categorize adulterants, and also "to determine their relation to digestion and health." But the fight was by no means over. A strong bill passed the House in 1903, but the Senate, preoccupied with statehood for Oklahoma, Arizona, and New Mexico, never got around to the food bill, and it died. But times were finally changing.

Political progressivism had begun to flower. Although the election of McKinley, a conservative, was a setback for the Populist movement, the growing discontent with the industrial age, its monopolies, its lobbies, and all the other dislocations of the hectic era, assured that progressivism would rise again. And the discontent had turned on some sectors of society with profound effect. Ida Tarbell took out after Standard Oil and its avaricious behavior. Ray Stannard Baker worked on the railroad's use and abuse of power. In every field, opposition to current trends arose in the form of books, magazine articles, speeches. Teddy Roosevelt, who was by no means averse to stirring things up himself, became so exasperated at the shrill voices lashing out in all directions that he called them a disparaging name that was to become part of the American lexicon—muckrakers.

At first, the food and drug industries got off rather easily. It was Wiley himself who finally borrowed a page from industry and came up with a gimmick to attract attention to his product—the "poison squad." In a brilliant burst worthy of any advertising man, Wiley chose twelve healthy, virile young men and systematically fed them adulterants morning, noon, and night. Independent studies had shown that in an average day's eating, an American consumer ingested 40 separate doses of questionable chemicals, and it was Wiley's stated intention to see what effect this had on the nation's health. The subtle effect of eating chemicals was largely beyond the precision of the era's scientists to determine, and Wiley never proved very much with his poison squads. But he got the nation to thinking.

First on the menu for the poison squad was boric acid, which in a massively documented report was found to "create disturbances of appetite, of digestion, and of health." Salycylic acid, sulphurous acid, benzoic acid, and formaldehyde followed in carefully measured doses. The response was unprecedented. An enterprising young reporter on *The Washington Post* ran a series of articles on the tests, and his original intention to be humorous gradually evolved into wild exaggeration that helped Wiley's cause greatly. *McClure's* and *Colliers Weekly*, two important publications of the day, issued a continuous stream of cogent, devastating editorials against excesses and insensitivity in the

food-processing industry. If the critics sometimes overstepped the
bounds of objectivity and fact, they could hardly be blamed.
When confronted with a candy-maker who added ground bone to
his shredded coconut goodies, and who tolerated no complaints
because "it don't hurt none," perhaps too much of a swing of the
pendulum in the other direction was necessary to redress the
balance.

The sensationalism that Wiley abhored began to have its
effect. Politics was evolving in his favor, too. Roosevelt, who had
become president after McKinley's assassination, called for an
attack on "serious social problems" in his inaugural address in
1900, and took his case over the heads of a recalcitrant Congress
with his offer to the people of a "Square Deal."

When Roosevelt was elected in his own right in 1904 by a
wide margin, he was able to pursue the cause of progressivism
more freely. His famous burst of "trust-busting" was more talk
than results, but the publicity fed the fires of social change. For
the first time since Jefferson, the quality of life, a phrase and
philosophy taken up half a century later by John F. Kennedy,
became an issue. Land reclamation and timber conservation
movements revealed the senseless waste of the nation's resources.
One baleful effect of the 1904 election, however, was that it
caused the death of yet another version of the food and drug bill.
"If a law like this goes into effect and is enforced just before a
Presidential election," said Representative James R. Mann of
Illinois, "so as to interfere with commercial business, it will have
a very deleterious effect on the party in power." In other words,
consumerism was considered bad politics—an attitude among
politicians that has only just begun to disappear.

The campaign against impure foods and dangerous drugs
built steadily. The Women's Christian Temperance Union took
out after the alcohol in patent medicines. Calls for proper labeling
of drugs alarmed the nation's druggists. The Proprietary Association of America warned that drug legislation "would practically
destroy the sale of proprietary remedies in the United States."
Industry was changing, though for its own reasons. The long fight
of the dairy interests against oleomargarine producers succeeded
in cordoning oleo off from the high-priced spread; but as a result,
the dairy industry ran out of reasons for opposing general food
laws and began to support them. On close inspection, such

legislation turned out to pose only minimal problems for reputable concerns.

On February 21, 1906, another bill passed the House. It was a weak bill, with no provision for setting standards of purity, no labeling of dangerous ingredients in drugs, no control over the curative claims made for nostrums. One requirement that Wiley considered almost tragic was that food-processors would be liable under the law only if they "knowingly" adulterated their products. Wiley knew that while ignorance of the law is no excuse, it makes an excellent defense in a trial. He pressed for a stronger bill in the Senate.

Assistance from outside kept mounting. *The Ladies Home Journal* and its editor Edward Bok upset the ladies of the land with tough and accurate articles. A long series in *Colliers* by Samuel Hopkins Adams finally turned the public against some of the more noxious nostrums in the drug stores.

But the bill didn't budge. It was "anti-business," philosophically unsound, and politically unsupportable. The thinking on the two sides was poles apart. In Wiley's mind, "the real evil of food adulteration is deception of the consumer." This attitude was not only rejected by the giants of the American commercial and industrial systems, but it was incomprehensible to them as an issue. The attitude was succinctly expressed by financier George Baker: "It's none of the public's business what I do." To be sure, the reputable companies of the day would not knowingly engage in criminal acts where food was concerned—poisoning the consumer was unwise because it was bad for the business. The same philosophy that would compel a cannery owner to avoid poisoning his customers also compelled him to put poisoning into his products—an off-color pea was bad business, but a pea tastefully colored with sublethal doses of copper sulphate was good business. The thought that the consumer had an inherent right not to be deceived never entered his mind. To call the use of adulterants a fraud was ridiculous.

In the end, what put the pure food and drug movement over these built-in barriers was not a change of heart. Suddenly, in the spring of 1906, impure and adulterated foods became bad business. Upton Sinclair, a hot-headed young socialist, set out to bring down the whole capitalistic system by revealing the inhuman exploitation of the workers by industry. To drive his point home, he chose workers who suffered not only from the insensitivity of their employees, but from the repulsive nature of their place of employ—the Chicago meat-packing houses. From his point of view, Sinclair's book, *The Jungle*, missed its mark. "I aimed for the nation's heart," he later said, "and hit its stomach instead." The book horrified an entire nation with its utterly revolting passages. It even ruined Teddy Roosevent's appetite, and he suggested that his Secretary of Agriculture read the book and determine whether the work of fiction was based on fact. Soon after, page proofs of three factual articles on the same subject arrived at the White House; they were studies done by Sinclair's publisher, and the facts were just as bad as the fiction. Roosevelt ordered an independent investigation, and on May 25, a strong meat-inspection law had been amended to the department's annual appropriations act.

The specific concern for pure meat quickly generalized into an overall consumer-protection movement led by the President himself. He began pushing the Senate-passed food and drug measure which was still lingering in the House. The people's lobby, such as the National Consumer's League and legions of large and small women's groups over the nation, flooded Congress with mail. Some Congressmen tried to water down the meat bill; Roosevelt responded by ordering the results of his independent investigation published. An attempt to permit packers to challenge Federal inspectors in court before any seizure could be carried out was defeated, a strong meat inspection bill passed the House, and was accepted by the Senate.

At the same time, the revitalized food and drug bill was reported out of committee on June 20, with provision for twelve hours of debate. Three days later, the bill passed by a vote of 241 to 17. It was an act of qualified courage on the part of the House—112 members did not vote. The strong House bill went to conference for reconciliation with the far weaker Senate version. The outcome was preordained. Pressure from the public and from state and local officials as well ended with the emergence of a reasonably strong bill. President Roosevelt signed both the meat Inspection Act and the Pure Food and Drug Act on June 30.

The meat bill resulted in step-by-step inspection of all meat that was to travel in interstate commerce, and is still the cornerstone of consumer protection in that field today. The food and drug bill, a far more complicated issue, had lost a few ingredients in conference, the most important being the loss of standards-setting powers for the government. But it gave the Agriculture Department power to proscribe preservatives it considered unsafe, and called for a distinction between straight whiskey and blends. It ruled that a food-processor need not "knowingly" adulterate his product to be liable to a fine, imprisonment, and seizure of his supplies; the bill made law of a long-resisted theory that the producer should be liable for all his acts whether he pleaded ignorance or not. The drug section of the bill provided some control over curative claims—that is, whether Dr. Johnson's Mild Combination Treatment for Cancer really could deliver on its promise. It also provided for improved labeling of drugs, particularly where substances such as cocaine, chloral hydrate, chloroform, and alcohol were included. All in all, it seemed that major victories had been won.

But they hadn't. A new battle immediately started up on establishing the provisions of the bill and on enforcement. Borax, formaldehyde, copper sulphate, and other preservatives were banned, with sodium benzoate permitted in small quantities. Other followup efforts were less successful, and in the many bitter fights, Wiley made the mistake of pushing too far, and Teddy Roosevelt got rather bored and exasperated with it all. Could *Karo* call its product corn syrup? True, it was a syrup, and it was extracted from corn, but its usual name was glucose. Wiley insisted on calling it glucose, saying that "corn syrup" made it sound to be something more than what it was. Said T.R. in a burst of temper: "You must make the manufacturers call a spade a spade, but don't make them call it a damn shovel." Corn syrup it remained, and the argument helped only to damage Wiley's standing. Wiley's opposition to saccharin was a larger tactical error. He believed that the artificial sweetener deceived the public, and he further considered it to be injurious. Roosevelt was outraged: "anyone who says saccharin is injurious is an idiot." It turned out that his physician gave it to the President every day.

The battle over whiskey-labeling dragged on for years, until under President Taft the phrase "neutral spirits" was finally chosen to set straight whiskeys apart from their less pure brethren. Other fights results in more serious setbacks. After a long court fight, the Supreme Court finally ruled that the act gave no power to the government over the curative claims made by drugs, and the quacks were back in business. Wiley's fight against *Coca-Cola*, which at the time did not reveal the presence of caffeine among its bubbles, was taken to court. Wiley, who had taken time out at the age of 67 to get married, spent his honeymoon at the *Coca-Cola* trial. He lost his case.

Wiley made such a fuss over so many issues in the years following passage of the act that he gradually alienated most of his colleagues. His only consistent source of support was the American press, which had adopted Wiley as a man of integrity and deep concern for the public. In 1912, Wiley finally resigned his post, leaving behind him an Agriculture Department populated with bureaucrats of considerably less zeal for the consumer's welfare. He also quit the Republican Party after a life of loyal support, and campaigned for the Democratic nominee, Woodrow Wilson, saying with all his considerable vigor that his former party was "so completely subjugated by the dollar, so permeated by the canker of big business as its only god, that only disastrous defeat can ever restore it to health." When Wilson won the election, he gave part of the credit for his victory to Wiley and the pure-food issue.

On balance, Wiley's career was a victorious one. He and his allies and the muckrakers created a purity-conscious public, and educated citizens to the ways of the industrial society. The long fight over the law's passage also accomplished one more critically important thing; it marked the beginning of the end for the doctrine of *caveat emptor*, and began the era of *caveat venditor*.

But the victory was neither complete nor permanent. Food and drug producers had had their activities circumscribed to a considerable degree. Many outrages were removed from the marketplace. Industry followed the letter of the law often only after a prolonged fight to weaken it or obstruct it, but seldom followed the spirit of the law. Given the nature of the system, a factory owner who chose to label his product completely and honestly, keep it pure, limit his advertising to the utter truth, and otherwise generally respect the rights of the purchaser could have survived in the highly competitive marketplace only by producing a clearly superior product at a competitive price. But high quality and complete honesty were among the more difficult and unpopular routes to financial success. Quality was just a factor in the cost equation. Honesty simply didn't sell, and had no chance to sell, in an essentially dishonest marketplace.

From 1906 on, government action in the marketplace became a series of half-steps designed to put the spirit of the Pure Food and Drug Act down on paper as the law of the land. In 1912, an amendment was tacked on to the bill prohibiting false and fraudulent claims for the curative and therapeutic effects of drugs. But the word "knowingly" crept back into the legislation, and promoters of the drugs found it relatively easy to hide behind a cloak of ignorance. A year later, one battle that Wiley had lost was finally won, when Congress required food-packages to reveal the quantity contained inside. Little else was done to sharpen and strengthen the law for three decades.

Technology meanwhile marched on, rapidly outdating the 1906 law. It had proscribed the use of certain preservatives then widely used, but proved ineffective against new ones that might come along. And come along they did. Food colors, too, required no clearance before use and the situation with coal-tar dyes— particularly with regard to the impurities often found in them—led to a voluntary arrangement with the government testing them at the expense of the maker and user. This hit-or-miss protection of the consumer from unsafe, impure, misbranded, and fradulent commodities on the storeshelf per-sisted until the 1930's, when a new wave of progressivism and populism swept the land.

Although the Pure Food and Drug Act and the Meat Inspection Act were the most dramatic attempts to protect the consumer of the early 20th Century, they struck more at the symptoms of a national ill than at the root cause. The doctrine of rugged individualism, good enough for the consumer, had long since been cast aside by industry as a bit too rugged for its own needs. The Panic of 1873 and other less drastic swings in the economic cycle, the vicious competition and cutthroat price wars, caused industry to go through an evolution that proceeded from gentleman's agreements on prices and markets to that most famous of all American economic inventions, the trust.

Standard Oil and John D. Rockefeller started it. The Oil Trust he formed in 1882 was composed of firms that had once competed with him, but now agreed to be operated as an economic unit by a board of trustees. The Oil Trust quickly dominated the nation's oil market, undercutting competition and absorbing it, buying out successful wildcatters. The trust worked eminently well at controlling the industry, and by the close of the century the United States sported a Steel Trust, Sugar Trust, a Tobacco Trust—300 industrial combinations all told, composed of 5,000 firms that once competed with one another.

In one sense, the effect of these combinations was salutary. Their size led to economies of scale, which lowered costs. Pricing policies, however, were generally determined by what the traffic would bear, and tremendous profits were pocketed by the trustees. Concentration in the economic arena and the drift away from the farm rapidly urbanized the nation, completing the collapse of the old agrarian society and replacing it with no society at all—the impersonal, anarchic world of the city wage-earner who had utterly no control over anything, from his wages to the prices he paid for the necessities of life.

The workers didn't like it much. Between 1881 and 1900 there were 24,000 strikes affecting 128,000 establishments. The Knights of Labor, which prospered until the Haymarket Riot in 1886 where an uninvited anarchist in an otherwise peaceful protest march tossed a bomb and killed seven policemen, gave way to the American Federation of Labor which counted 500,000 members by 1900. The A.F. of L. fought for an eight-hour day and a six-day work week, opposed child labor (on economic rather than humanitarian grounds) and pressed for higher pay. But the union was open to skilled laborers only, and perhaps one in ten American workers qualified for membership. The rest of society was not organized. The consumer was still a rugged individualist, like it or not.

Obviously, the thought occurred to some social observers that the old doctrine of *laissez-faire* was not serving the industrial society's citizens well at all. Henry C. Adams, a University of Michigan economist, suggested in 1897 that the new system of economics required "a new system of ethics, a new expression of rights and duties, indeed a new definition of liberty and of the individual himself... Under the old individualistic rules of industry, morality centered in the individual life. No opportunity was presented for the evolution of social ethics, no necessity for testing motives by their social results." With the advent of the progressive era, this revolutionary notion that industrial performance must be balanced by the social costs of an action in the marketplace began to take hold. A large part of this new philosophy came from the farm belt, where Populism had its roots, for the farmer was being steamrollered by events in the cities. A commentator on the scene wrote in 1889: "The agricultural masses. . .are robbed by an infamous system of finance; they are plundered by transportation companies; they are imposed upon by unjust systems of tariff laws; they are deprived of their lands and other property by an iniquitous system of usury; they are fleeced by the exactions of numerous trusts; they are preyed upon by the merchants, imposed upon by the lawyers, misled by the politician and seem to be regarded as the legitimate prey of all other classes. Monopoly names the price of what they have to sell, and charges then what it pleases for what they are compelled to buy. . . Individual effort is fruitless."

The heavy toll exacted on farmers by the railroads had already led to one attempt to create a more orderly marketplace. The Interstate Commerce Commission had been formed in 1887 with a mandate to regulate rates and watchdog practices of the industry. The individual consumer was at best a silent partner in the passage of the act; essentially it was a contest between factions, won primarily because although the railroads had more money in their pockets, the farmers had more Senators and Congressmen in theirs.

Three years later, what might be considered the first attempt to work a fundamental change in the structure and function of the marketplace was made, when the Sherman anti-trust act passed. Again, the law was designed to protect one faction against another faction, in this case the small entrepreneur against the giant combination that regularly squeezed all competition out of the marketplace. So brazen was the operation of the Oil Trust in fixing prices, controlling the market, and generally running its corner of the economy like some malevolent despot that the Sherman Act's language was made very specific. It declared illegal "every contract, combination in the form of trust or otherwise, or conspiracy, in restraint of trade or commerce among the several states, or with foreign nations." The power to regulate commerce among the several states had been granted Congress by Article I of the Constitution, and the exercise of that right in the Sherman Act seemed direct, straightforward, and unequivocal. But it didn't work out that way. Another branch of government, the Supreme Court, decided that the nature of the American economy was a matter for its consideration and judgment. In 1890, the Court had overturned a Minnesota statute which gave a state commission authority over railroad rates, stating that "the question of reasonableness of a rate of charge. . .is eminently a question for judicial determination." A corporation, which had already been ruled to be a "person" by the court just as much as any individual was, and thus protected by the Fourteenth amendment's due process of law clause, could thus not be deprived of its property (in this case its charges for its property) simply by statute. In effect, the court set up the nation's judicial machinery as final arbiter of the government's efforts to regulate the economy. And it happened that the Supreme Court of the nineteenth century's last decade took a very narrow and conservative view of things.

When the first court test of the Sherman Act came in 1895, the Sugar Trust case, there was no question that the sugar refiners had entered into a monopolistic combination, that they were charging unfair prices, and were generally restraining trade. But, said the Court, the Sugar Trust is primarily engaged in manufacturing, which is an intrastate operation. Its raw materials were imported, crossing both national and state boundaries, and its final product recrossed the lines on the way to the marketplace, but that didn't make the sugar business an interstate affair. It was primarily a local operation, the court ruled, and therefore not within the jurisdiction of the Sherman Act. The logic is astounding by present standards. In 1949, the Supreme Court finally got around to saying that "if it is interstate commerce that feels the pinch, it does not matter how local the operation which applies the squeeze."

The ruling left the Sherman Act in tatters. Years later, in 1905, the Court retraced its steps somewhat when the Beef Trust came before the tribunal. This time the balance on the court had tipped the other way for the moment, and Justice Oliver Wendell Holmes narrowed the distinction between direct or indirect involvement in interstate commerce. Although meat processing went on solely within the state, the cattle came from elsewhere, and the beef was sold throughout the land. That was enough for Holmes. "Its effect upon commerce among the States is not accidental, secondary, remote, or merely probable. . .the subject matter is sales and the very point of the combination is to restrain and monopolize commerce among the States in respect of such sales."

But the larger battle as far as the consumer was concerned was whether the courts had a proper role in shaping the economy. Holmes thought not. He felt it was a social matter for determination by the legislature, and ultimately by the people through the polls, and not for determination by the courts. "A constitution," he wrote, "is not intended to embody a particular economic theory, whether of paternalism and the organic relation of the citizen to the State or of *laissez-faire*." He proposed "judicial restraint." The classic case demonstrating that such restraint was not to be exercised came in 1905. The court struck down a New York State law restricting working hours in bakeries to ten hours a day and sixty hours a week. The state, it said, had no right to interfere with a bakery worker's liberty and his freedom to contract. If he wanted to work a hundred hours in a 100-degree bakery, that was his private affair. "There must be more than the mere fact of the possibility of some small amount of unhealthiness to warrant legislative interference with liberty," the court ruled. Justice Holmes' dissenting view that bakeries were none of the court's business, and strictly up to the state, went unheeded.

The Pure Food and Drug Act of 1906 managed to squeeze by the Court as a proper exercise of the government's police power, but in the consumer's exercise of his political power, he found himself restrained by the court's warmhearted but misplaced concern for his individual liberty. Liberty was still defined by many as the absence of government.

The Court's most infamous action of the era was undoubtedly its ruling against Standard Oil, now altered from a trust to a holding company. The court agreed that the company was a combination which restrained trade—not by the rules of the Sherman Act, though, but by something called the "rule of reason." After many years in the limbo of dissenting opinion

Justice Edward Douglass White suddenly found himself in the majority with his observation that restraints of trade were illegal only if they were unreasonable. "Reasonable" restraints of trade were all right. Thus the court set itself up once again as the final arbiter in the evolution—or lack of evolution—of the marketplace. There were, according the Justice White's theory, good trusts and bad trusts. Standard Oil, it was agreed, was a bad trust. U.S. Steel, which had become the first billion-dollar operation in the U.S. in 1904 when it swallowed up most of the U.S. steel-producing capacity, was ruled to be a good trust in 1920.

The ruling caused considerable consternation in Congress, to say the least, where the legislative branch had witnessed itself overruled. To be sure, size itself does not necessarily restrain trade or injure the public; at least, it does not have to. The fact that it virtually always did in the early days of monopoly and holding companies perhaps escaped notice. Teddy Roosevelt announced that he was "against misconduct, not against wealth," a position which allied itself with the rule of reason—and against the mood of the nation. The mantle of progressivism had fallen from his shoulders, passing to another president, Woodrow Wilson.

Shortly after the ruling was made, Congress attempted to move control of the industrial state from the judiciary back to the legislature. The Senate Committe on Commerce began hearings in 1911. Two years and five volumes of testimony later, the committee called for a new law on restraint of trade, and on suppression of competition. Wilson meanwhile campaigned on an anti-monopoly ticket. Competition was an important ingredient to the American way, he felt, as long as it was "competition that fights fair." He, together with Louis Brandeis, resisted Roosevelt's concept and called for laws outlawing unfair competition and penalizing any actions which had the intent of creating a monopoly. The package was part of his "New Freedom," and the doctrine was spelled out in this manner by a political scientist in 1912. . ."Widely organized and directed state action not only enlarges the moral, physical and intellectual capacities of individuals, but increases their liberty of action by removing obstacles placed in their way by the strong and self-seeking. In truth the state emancipates and promotes as well as restrains." Wilson put it more briefly in a campaign speech: "Property is an instrument of humanity; humanity isn't an instrument of property." He called for a qualitative change in the relationship of industry to the people, an end to the Gospel of Wealth.

Wilson's plan was two-fold. First, he called for a new law to strengthen the Sherman Act. Second, he recommended the creation of a Federal Trade Commission "as an indispensable instrument of information and publicity" but with little power. The FTC Act that Congress generated paralleled Wilson's suggestion, and the Clayton Act gave the government power to move against any acts which lessened competition. But the language was so fuzzy and unclear that even the business world began pressing for a clearer set of regulations. At the last minute a Presidential aide, George Rublee, teamed up with New Hampshire Congressman Raymond Stevens to take the control of unfair competitive practice out of the Clayton Act and put it into the FTC Act. With the help of Wilson, their plan was finally adopted by a House-Senate conference.

Despite its last-minute dash into existence, the plan was ingenious. The experience of the Sherman Act had shown that full-blown legal assaults on monopolies and unfair practices were too slow. The FTC, now empowered to move against "unfair methods of competition" with cease and desist orders could, in theory, move quickly and surely to nip monopolistic practices in the bud. The lowest citizen could also find a sympathetic ear at the commission, where under the original Clayton Act he would have needed the power or resources to sue a billion-dollar operation. And the FTC could weigh each individual case on its particular merits, without being forced to come up with some sweeping definition of "unfairness" that was still precise enough to stop individual offenders quickly. The Clayton Act, meanwhile, was left with power to move against such classic evils as rebates, interlocking directorates, exclusive sales contracts, and price cutting designed to kill competition. It also specifically exempted labor unions from regulations against combinations, legalized peaceful strikes, picketing, and boycotts. These measures corrected one of the more ironic aftereffects of the Sherman Act; its first success was against a union, not against industry.

The package seemed ideal—one major act to move with the full force of government against illegal restraints of trade, and a commission to act on a less exalted level, serving as a first line of defense against incipient trusts, and building up a body of administrative law which would gradually come to serve as guidelines for industry. But it soon became clear that the means of redressing the balance between the buyer and the seller, between industry and the people, had not yet been found. In 1919, the Supreme Court again assumed a supra-legislative role, throwing out a case brought by the FTC. The Commission had moved against two brothers named Gratz who sold ties that were used to bind up cotton bales—but would not sell the ties unless the buyers also bought six yards of bagging to encase the bales. The FTC thought that was unfair. The Court said that "the words 'unfair method of competition' are not defined by the statute, and their exact meaning is in dispute. It is for the courts, not the commission, ultimately to determine. . .what they include." And the FTC had shown no "ability, purpose, or intent" on the part of the brothers to acquire a monopoly. "If real competition is to continue," said the Court, "the right of the individual to exercise reasonable discretion in respect of his own business must be preserved." The doctrine of *caveat emptor* was dying hard.

In an eloquent dissent, Justice Brandeis futilely explained to his brethren the philosophy of the FTC Act. The phrase "unfair methods of competition," he said, meant any method that might be put to an unfair end, if not in this case, then in another circumstance. He thought that the common practice of tying products together and forcing the buyer to take the whole deal or nothing should be stopped on the grounds that it was inherently unfair. He explained that the FTC was a new device created by Congress "in the hope thereby of remedying conditions in business which a great majority of the American people regarded as menacing the general welfare, and which, for more than a generation, they have vainly attempted to remedy by the ordinary procedures of law." His arguments were wasted; the FTC shrank into insignificance.

With the coming of the war and America's entry into it, other preoccupations took precedence, and by 1917, the Progressive Era and the evolution it sought to force had run its course, and lay dormant for more than a decade.

The marketplace remained essentially unchanged in its day-to-day operation, and the processes of industrialization and urbanization had been completed. By 1920, more than half of the population lived in urban areas, and 72 per cent were engaged in non-agricultural pursuits. Economic concentration had proceeded despite the anti-monopoly activity; half of the output of industry was generated by a shade more than one per cent of the concerns in existence. In practical terms, John D. Rockefeller was right in 1904 when he said that "the day of combination is here to stay. Individualism is gone, never to return."

But the seeds had been sown. By 1917, the government had firmly established its role in watchdogging the economy and protecting the public against excesses and unfair practices in the marketplace. And many legal actions were successful to help balance the disasters of the sugar trust case and other such backward steps. Price fixing, dividing markets and allocating customers, many forms of vertical and horizontal arrangements and conspiracies between firms—many such practices were outlawed. Federal inspectors walked the floors of meat-processing plants, checked the patent medicine's label, snooped on the marketing manager's latest plan to increase sales. In sum, the American industrial society was no longer completely unfettered, but circumscribed by a body of laws and a growing public awareness of its shortcomings. Between the seller and the buyer, though, it was still no contest. The buyer's victories were few, his knowledge of the marketplace diminished, his opinion merely something to be shaped to meet the needs of the hungry giant.

Battlegrounds Revisited

chapter 3

To say that the forces of reform became dormant after World War I is a massive understatement. The forces were buried under an avalanche of prosperity and tremendous national growth. The old order thrived in an "Era of Normalcy," while from the hibernating consumer leagues to the Justice Department's anti-trust division, which was slumbering along on annual appropriations of $250,000, voices of warning were seldom heard.

The second round in the consumer's rebellion was born out of the violent death of this Era of Normalcy. And it was more successful than the first round that ended with World War I. But by the time World War II came and ended the second round, the consumer was, practically speaking, worse off than ever. Despite the fact that the old order did everything it could to kill itself off with the Great Depression, the new order had neither the knowledge, the power, or the program to fill the vacuum.

The post-war period began inauspiciously. It was the time of the Palmer raids, when the Justice Department's Anti-Radical division under J. Edgar Hoover arrested dissidents of every coloration in midnight raids and shipped them out of the country. It was the era of Sacco and Vanzetti, two avowed radicals, arrested and convicted of murder on poor evidence and abysmal judicial procedure, and finally executed. New forces of reform included the Ku Klux Klan, resurrected during the war with Catholics and Jews added to Negroes on its list of undesirables.

With the arrival of Warren G. Harding in the White House in 1924 (an event which led him to exclaim: "My God, but this is a hell of a place for a man like me to be!") part of the United States government started practicing its own brand of free enterprise. To Harding goes the record for having appointed the only cabinet officer ever sent to prison for malfeasance in office—his Secretary of the Interior's profiteering in the Teapot Dome scandal. Between the total impotence of the government and the paranoid mood of the era, it was hardly the atmosphere for "socialism" and "welfare statism," which consumerism seemed to represent. Upton Sinclair, who a generation before had been a national hero, was now reduced to an unsuccesful candidate for public office.

Except for the liquor industry, which was ruled immoral and illegal by three-fourths of the states in 1920, American business never had it so good, and the American citizen did quite well, too. Prices held stable, even if wages failed to go up, and the purchasing power of the dollar climbed thirteen per cent from 1922 to 1927.

But socially, T.S. Eliot called it a time of "shape without form. . .gesture without motion." F. Scott Fitzgerald called the people "the lost generation." And when the material world collapsed in 1929, the nation was left with nothing of substance to support it during the greatest crisis in its history.

Herbert Hoover suddenly saw the world he understood and had once helped to manage go up in smoke, and neither he, Congress, nor the nation knew what to do about it. With the possible exception of John Maynard Keynes in England, whose theories of economics were promising but puzzling, there was hardly a social or economic thinker who knew what to do. The socialists, thoroughly ground down by anti-radical fervor, offered nothing that anyone wanted to listen to. The forces for reform had no battle plan. But they had a long list of complaints which began to find a new audience as the end of the boom years approached.

Two years before the crash, at a time when consumer groups abounded in the land but did little more than nip at the heels of local shopkeepers, a book appeared on the scene. An accountant-economist named Stuart Chase, together with mechanical engineer Frederick Schlink, wrote *"Your Money's Worth."* "Why do you buy one make of automobile rather than another? . . .Why do you buy the toothpaste you are using. . .? Is this cake of soap really going to give you a schoolgirl complexion?" Those were the sort of questions the book asked, and the answers it gave were both fascinating and disturbing, with their strong implication that the American public was being systematically suckered. *Listerine*, the book complained, did nothing but "cover one smell with another." *Lifebuoy's* magic passport to social acceptability was revealed to be creosol, a disinfectant highly recommended by the government for use in barns and chicken coops. In vivid language wherever possible, the book went on endlessly, and it quickly became a bible for the consumer movement with causes and tea-time tidbits on every page. Prof. Robert S. Lynd, author of the Middletown books which chronicled the emptiness of American life, called it "the Uncle Tom's Cabin of the consumer movement." Its impact was vast because its contents were novel to a generation of consumers who had been largely content to judge the social worth of the industrial society by the daily climb of their stockholdings.

The second wave of the consumer movement in the United States can be dated from the publication of *Your Money's Worth*. Its sales of over 100,000 copies restated a point learned a generation before—whether or not muckraking is successful, it attracts a wide audience and has a ready market, which was soon being tapped anew by magazine writers and book-publishers. As the news was circulated once again that business was somewhat unconcerned about its consumers, with an ample supply of examples to document the point, new pressures began to build for another round of government action to bring order to the marketplace.

The publication of the book also led to creation of a new institution of public interest—the consumer research organization. Schlink had formed a small consumer group in White Plains, N.Y., and within two years of the publications of his book, it had evolved into Consumer's Research, Inc. CR's purpose was to give the consumer an objective evaluation of the products in the marketplace by testing and rating goods, then publishing the results in a monthly magazine. Fiercely independent, non-profit, uncontaminated by ads in its magazine, CR grew rapidly.

Four years later, Schlink teamed with an officer of CR, a lean, dark, soft-spoken writer named Arthur Kallet, to write the most famous of all consumer tracts, *100,000,000 Guinea Pigs.* The book was virulent and unrelenting. "A hundred million Americans," the introduction to the first chapter began, "act as unwitting test animals in a gigantic experiment with poisons, conducted by the food, dairy, and cosmetic manufacturers." It went on to castigate many of the most popular and successful products of the day. The classic, the case of a German army officer who committed suicide by eating a tubeful of *Pebeco* toothpaste (it had enough potassium chlorate, said the authors, to kill three people) became a symbol of industrial insensitivity to the needs, cares, and even the lives of the public. Many of the cases dealt with fly-by-night operations, but many hit at the big names of American commerce and trade with baldly stated examples of their unconcern. Not a single lawsuit was filed against the authors for unjustly defaming a product; the notoriety of a trial would have just made matters worse, and the business community hoped that the storm would soon pass. But it didn't. The New Deal had just been born.

Franklin D. Roosevelt's election to the presidency had come amid the resurrected notion that the relationship between industry and its society was in need of repairing, that the American tradition which business professed to preserve was a self-serving fiction. Charles A. Beard, one of the most famous and free-swinging historians of the day, tried to bury the still-dominant philosophy of rugged individualism. "From day to day," he wrote in 1931, "it becomes increasingly evident that some of our economic leaders (by no means all of them) are using the phrase as an excuse for avoiding responsibility, for laying the present depression on 'government interference,' and for seeking to escape from certain forms of taxation and regulation which they do not find to their interest. If a smoke screen big enough can be laid on the land, our commercial prestidigitators may work wonders—for themselves. . ." In his typical blunt fashion, Beard added: "The cold truth is that the individualist creed of everybody for himself and the devil take the hindmost is principally responsible for the distress in which Western civilization finds itself—with investment racketeering at one end and labor racketeering at the other. Whatever merits the creed may have had in days of primitive agriculture and industry, it is not applicable in an age of technology, science, and rationalized economy."

With no body of modern industrial philosophy to draw on, all that FDR could do was assemble a "brains trust" and begin searching for a new way. Legend has it that FDR read of the Kallet-Schlink book and ordered Rexford Guy Tugwell, one of the members of his brains trust, to draft a bill strengthening the 1906 food and drug act. Whatever the origin of the plan, Tugwell did ask the chief of the Food and Drug Administration, Walter Campbell, to draft a bill. The Tugwell bill, as the first version was called, was a tough bill indeed. It would have banned all advertisements that were misleading even if only by ambiguity, and the Secretary of Agriculture would have been given sweeping powers over the manufacture and sale of foods, drugs, and cosmetics. The Tugwell bill started a battle that took five years to be resolved. The president of the Proprietary Association was among the most offended, because it was an "attempt to take away from the people the right of self-medication."

While the FDA went on the road with a chamber of horrors show composed of quack cures and dangerous nostrums, the depression-borne zeal of the consumer spread to other areas. The pet cause of consumer groups of the time was food-grading. Industry had had a scare in 1931 when a law requiring the labeling of foods below "standard" quality was passed, but without any breakdown of food grades above minimum quality. With the advent of the New Deal, however, the American consumer's existence was at last officially recognized with the creation of the Consumer's Advisory Board. Armed with the knowledge that industry bought its produce from farmers according to an A-B-C grading system, and reinforced by the presence of a similar retail grading system in neighboring Canada, the CAB attempted to institute a grading system in the American food industry.

Not that there weren't grading systems already in use. Rice was graded, for example, as extra fancy, fancy, extra choice,

choice or medium. Canned mushrooms topped all other entries in the labeling race with extra miniature, sur extra petite, sur extra, extra petite, extras, first choice, choice pieces, and stems. Any consumer who knew that "first choice" was third from the bottom in the grading system was probably either a mycologist or an employee of the Agriculture Department.

But the CAB had as many troubles of its own. Its parent, the NRA, was declared unconstitutional. The CAB bounced from agency to agency, landing in the Labor Department in 1935, until its statute ran out in 1938, when its work was passed on to the consumers council of the Agricultural Adjustment Administration, another New Deal creation. It never succeeded in its labeling campaign except in one area—dog food. One major advance did come out of the battle, though; some retailers, most notably A&P, instituted a practice of voluntary grading, either with a letter code or with the more or less descriptive adjectives "fancy," "choice," and "standard." There today is still no mandatory grading system in the U.S., but much of the food on supermarket shelves, particularly meat, is graded under a voluntary system using grading standards established by the government and executed by Federal inspectors. Three-fifths of the beef sold today is graded for the consumer. Much canned food is also packed under a consumer grading system, but the grade is seldom indicated on the can. As a recent Department of Agriculture publication tactfully puts it: "The commercial firm. . .does not wish to distract attention from its brand name by also using the U.S. grademark on the package." *Caveat emptor.*

The major battles of the 1930's were fought over attempts to strengthen and modernize the two landmark pieces of consumer-protection legislation passed a generation before—the FTC Act and the Pure Food and Drug Act. The latter was in tatters thanks to adverse court rulings and advances in technology. Dr. Wiley's act had for example ruled out the more deadly food additives of the day, but was ineffective against new ones that would inevitably come along. The situation was so potentially dangerous that industry in one case put itself under voluntary government clearance procedures with coal-tar derivatives. But the Tugwell bill and its successors seemed destined to sail the legislative seas without ever reaching shore, until an event horrified the nation. In 1937, the patent medicine known as *Elixir Sulfanilimide*, was marketed. The medicine, based on the new and potent sulfa family of wonder drugs, was safe enough in capsule form. But a company chemist, pressed to develop a liquid form, chose diethylene glycol as a solvent. More than 100 people died from the drug. The chemist shot himself.

Ironically, the tragedy occurred in an area which no one had yet thought to cover in the new bills. A new and historic section was quickly written, stating that no drug should be placed on the market until the manufacturer had proved to the satisfaction of the FDA that it was safe. This novel idea arose too late for the victims of *Elixir Sulfanilimide*, but just in time for the rest of the nation. Virtually all of the drugs in use today, many of them powerful and dangerous if not understood and used properly, did not even exist 30 years ago. The succeeding years were to prove that many more safeguards would be necessary to make drug safety a medical reality rather than just a legislative demand, but the proposed regulation served as the foundationstone for the future. It recognized that the consumer could not be protected by the traditional process of dragging careless or unscrupulous drug-makers to court after the fact. However at variance with the doctrine of *laissez-faire* the government's demand for control over the marketability of a new product might be, there clearly was no other choice for the society as a whole to make. As far as the drug industry was concerned, pretesting new drugs before they go to the marketplace was both good philosophy and good business—as the makers of the sulfanilimide brew had learned.

Thus a fundamental change had taken place in legislation. The Federal Food, Drug, and Cosmetic Act passed Congress in 1938, and it was a preventive law, where its predecessor was primarily a punitive one that punished the offender after the fact. The new version of the act recognized that the consumer had indeed become a guinea pig for the testing of new products, procedures, and processes, and took at least some steps to halt such goings-on. It extended the FDA's domain to cosmetics and medical devices. The previously voluntary arrangements for certification of coal-tar dyes used in cosmetics as well as food were made mandatory. The new act flatly proscribed the addition of any poisonous or deleterious substance to foodstuffs except where absolutely necessary, and then within strictly controlled limits—an approach which had been considered an outrageous violation of the industry's freedom three decades earlier. Factory inspections by federal agents were made mandatory in establishments processing foods, drugs, cosmetics and shipping them in interstate commerce. Most important, a precedent-setting provision gave the FDA the power to obtain court injunctions against the sale of products it deemed a threat to the nation's health. This large dose of preventive medicine in the food and drug industry was without doubt a major victory for the consumer. He even succeeded in getting some degree of grading and labeling requirements imposed on the food industry.

But the grading regulation was minimal, merely drawing a line between standard and substandard food, and the rest of the act had loopholes big enough to drive a meat truck through. All the classic reasons apply—pressure from lobbies, captive Congressmen, and something short of full attention by the Administration. It is clear in retrospect that a major problem was ignorance, on all sides of the debate. A complete and heavily-endorsed philosophy of the marketplace was being altered, and those who sought to alter it were inventing as they went along. The concept of a Federal role in predetermining the safety of a drug seems preposterously simple now. Then it was fraught with implications that no one could quite grasp. Without a heavy dose of national emotion from the sulfanilimide disaster to help it, it probably would not have gotten through.

The notion of government planning also disturbed many who looked around them and saw large chunks of their world turning socialist and, worse, communist. The very word "planning" was becoming a dirty word, smacking of those anticapitalist notions of foreign economists and political philosophers who used America as their example of a decadent society unworthy of continued existence. The consumer was also questioning the American way in the marketplace and the economy, often with the same words. Arthur Kallet, for example, quite honestly told a reporter he hoped the Soviet style of economics would succeed, and that the American economic system was going out of style. His talk made him quite unpopular in some quarters. Besides, he was a troublemaker at Consumer's Research, Inc.

That hard-driving outfit was ahead of its time in every sense except one—its own labor relations. Its employees were underpaid, overworked, denied the right to bargain collectively, and were summarily fired if they made too much of a fuss. In the summer of 1935, Kallet and half of the employees of CR marched out the door and went on strike. "It was no dialectical schism," *Scribner's* magazine observed two years later, "no paper maneuver, but a bloody, head-bashing, rock-throwing, car-wrecking strike—for its size probably as violent as any labor dispute ever seen in this country."

The dispute went all the way to the National Labor Relations Board where CR and its head Arthur Schlink were overruled. But in the meantime Kallet had walked all the way out and set up a new organization, Consumers Union. The new organization and its magazine, *Consumer Reports*, was an instant, and an enduring, success.

CU passed CR in subscriptions within three years. It also outstripped its predecessor in what it told the consumer. The products of American concerns were rated—and so were their labor policies, a practice which by implication at least suggested boycotts. CU was quickly branded a Stalinist publication by some quarters.

The suspicion that communism was involved in the American consumer movement of the late 1930s was not all in the imaginations of its critics. Just as in the labor movement, the Cummunist party did try to move in on the movement, in some cases setting up its own consumer organizations to spread discontent. It was good Marxist-Leninist theory that largely flopped—there just weren't that many consumers in the U.S. who were interested in overthrowing the whole government in order to keep the bugs out of their food. Nevertheless, the Communist interest in consumerism earned the movement a Congressional investigation by Martin Dies and the House Un-American Activities Committee.

On December 10, 1939, the committee released a long report prepared by its research director. The Communist party, the report stated, was busily employing the "Trojan Horse" technique of setting up new organizations and penetrating existing ones in all fields. "Scores of so-called consumer organizations became involved in this Communist tactic," the report continued, "organizations newly created by the Communist party ostensibly for the purpose of serving the interests of consumers, as well as existing organizations which were in fact, devoted to legitimate consumer interest." Fourteen consumer groups were listed. Among them was Consumers Union, which was born out of the "agitation and maneuvering of the Communist party." Kallet's "political connections" were blended in with his "typically Communist comment," including his opposition to the profit system which he felt led to excesses in the marketplace, and his praise of the Soviet system's economic theories.

The research director who wrote the report was J.B. Matthews, himself a converted "fellow-traveler"—and once an officer of Consumer's Research who remained on the company side of the picket line and fought against Kallet and the strikers. Nothing much came of the attack on Kallet and CU. The charge had been heard before, and even the critics of Kallet classified him somewhat acidly as a "professor of perfection" rather than a conspirator bent on overthrowing the government. Kallet and CU were hardly affected by the investigation. Both are alive and well today, with CU still pronouncing its "best buys" and "not acceptables" over the entire range of consumer products, and Kallet running a publication that concentrates on the drug industry.

The laws Kallet helped create prospered, too, relatively speaking. The courts had already begun to take a more liberal view of the intent of consumer legislation. In 1924, for example, a court dryly observed that "it is not difficult to choose statements, designs and devices which will not deceive," but it usually took years to have the spirit of the law affirmed as well as its letter. In one of the first cases contested under the 1938 act, a retail druggist was prosecuted for selling sulfa pills without a prescription. The purchasers were usually treating themselves for gonorrhea, and authorities objected not only because of the hazards of the drug, but because improper treatment could lead to development of medication-resistant strains, thereby worsening an already serious public health problem.

The druggist's conviction was overturned by a court of appeals, on grounds that sales of the product took place within a state, and therefore was not embraced by the interstate-commerce clause of the Federal constitution. The Supreme Court, however, upheld the conviction in a precedent-setting case. It ruled that the purpose of the 1938 drug act "was to safeguard the consumer by applying its requirements to articles from the moment of their introduction into interstate commerce all the way to the moment of their delivery to the ultimate consumer." Many narrow and narrow-minded interpretations of this and other pieces of consumer-protection legislation fell by the wayside with that ruling. But the ruling came in 1948, a full ten years after the act had passed.

Sometimes, it took more than a consumer-minded ruling by the courts to eliminate obvious weaknesses in the food and drug marketplaces. In one case involving the contamination of macaroni and spaghetti by rats in a warehouse, a court ruled that the Federal law did not apply, since the food had already ended its passage through interstate commerce and was now purely under the jurisdiction of the state. Again, the trouble took ten years to correct; in 1948 an amendment flatly extended Federal jurisdiction to all products shipped in interstate commerce, right up to their final sale to a consumer. (In 1961, a court ruled that a product manufactured and sold within a single state was covered, too, if any of its ingredients came from out-of-state.)

For years after the passage of the act, Congress found—and is still finding—it necessary to plug the holes in the law. Sometimes the action came just in the nick of time. In 1941, Congress suddenly became aware that insulin, a drug that meant life or death to its users, was about to emerge from its protective patent held by the University of Toronto. The resultant flood of insulin on the market from new and variously qualified manufacturers could have meant life and death indeed for the diabetics who use it. Too weak in strength, and the drug would permit blood-sugar to rise to the point where fatal convulsions could occur. Too strong a dose could mean insulin shock. One day before the patent was to expire, a law was signed providing for prior testing and standardization of all insulin placed on the market.

The "wonder drugs" that appeared on the civilian market after World War II, led by penicillin, are now under similar legislation, but it took Congress nearly two decades to complete the job. First, penicillin was subjected to batch testing and certification by the FDA in 1945. As new antibiotics appeared, Congress had to pass another law to include them in the same jurisdiction. Streptomycin was brought under Federal control in 1947. In 1949, aureomycin, chloramphenicol and bacitracin required another new Act of Congress. Finally, in 1962, Congress grew tired of retracing its steps and ruled that all antibiotics would automatically fall under control of the FDA.

Fortunately, many of the loopholes were closed before another tragedy occurred. But not always. And at least once, the trouble occurred even though Federal laws covered the situation. A red food dye covered by the 1938 color-additive clause and subsequently certified harmless caused legions of Halloween trick-or-treaters to become ill in 1950. Luckily, there were no deaths, but the incident made all those concerned realize anew that technology as well as legislation had to be kept up with the times. As a result of the incident, all coal-tar dyes were re-evaluated. Some were found to cause illness in laboratory animals when ingested in large quantities. A commonly-used lipstick coloring was banned. Another dye used to deepen the hue of oranges, presumably on the theory that they would look more like oranges if nature's work were improved upon, was also banned. Industry thereupon proceeded to develop whole new families of coloring about whose purity there could be no doubt. Coal-tar dyes were largely dropped as a bad idea on principle. In this case, the law had actually backfired by stifling technological innovation—coal-tar dyes were certified by the government, and therefore industry naturally enough was content with them.

The 1938 law had many weaknesses, but perhaps it is unfair to criticize it too heavily. It did establish further the right of the government to intrude upon private property—the manufacturer— in order to protect the public interest. To a certain extent, it gave the FDA and other agencies charged with its enforcement the power to stop novel dangers and deceptions from remaining in the marketplace, without having to dash to Congress for an amendment or run all the way to the Supreme Court in an interminable piece of litigation. Its gaps often represented the limits of understanding of those who created the law as well as holes deliberately shot in it by its opponents. But the law could hardly be called the last word in consumer protection. At the least, one more hard-fought round would be needed before it could be said that drugs on the market were properly labeled. One more fight would be required before they could be pronounced effective as well as safe, and worth the money consumers spent on them. And one more tragedy, this one the worst of all because it disfigured its victims for life, would be required to prove once and for all that no amount of prior review of a new drug was too much.

The New Deal contributed other forms of consumer protection, some of major significance. The Federal Trade Commission, which had languished in the 1920's for lack of funds, talent, and the proper words in its legislation, scored one major victory right off the bat. The first of the so-called "truth" bills (it was the first and only such bill for 33 years) passed in 1933. Under the Truth in Securities act, all stocks and other securities traded in interstate commerce had to be registered with the FTC, and information about them had to be accurate. Criminal penalties were provided in case the shady speculations of the boom years were repeated. This new-found power and responsibility of the FTC lasted only one year. In 1934, the Securities and Exchange Commission was created and given broad powers to regulate the stock and bond markets. Together with the Banking Act of 1933, which severely limited the forms of investing and speculating banks could practice, the two acts went a long way toward protecting the consumer's attempts to enjoy the benefits of capitalism directly.

The FTC had other fish it was trying to hook, though. It had found that the phrase "unfair methods of competition" was too narrow—at least in the court's mind—to catch whole classes of ills in the marketplace. A classic case illustrates the problem. *Marmola* was a popular weight-reducing compound of no medical merit whatsoever. It was popular because it was heavily advertised. The FTC issued a cease and desist order against *Marmola's* makers, on grounds that its ads were false and misleading. The case went all the way to the Supreme Court, where, the Court agreed, the ads were indeed false. However, the Court added, that didn't mean the company was employing an unfair method of competition. The FTC's case was thrown out, and *Marmola* continued to be sold.

Whether the ruling or the FTC act was the deficient organ was a moot point; the FTC began a long compaign to gain control over advertising. So did the FDA. Consumer leaders generally sided with the FDA. The consumerists lost, but the consumer movement scored a major victory in 1938 when the Wheeler-Lea Act gave to the FTC powers to move against "unfair trade practices." Now all manner of misleading and deceptive advertising and market practices could be brought to a halt with some degree of speed. In the case of food, drugs and cosmetics, any deliberately misleading advertising, particularly of a potentially harmful product, could be speedily halted by injunction. Thus the act of 1914 was changed from one which aided the consumer indirectly by ruling out sharp practices between businessmen, to one which directly aided the consumer. In terms of marketplace philosophy, little more could have been asked.

Even the Supreme Court was changing its attitudes toward business behavior. President Roosevelt, thoroughly frustrated by the adverse rulings of the Court on two of his major New Deal recovery instruments, the National Industrial Recovery Act and the Agricultural Adjustment Act, tried to remake the Court by increasing its size or inducing some of its nine old men to retire. Congress killed his plan, but Associate Justice Owen J. Roberts, the junior man on the bench at 61, chose that moment, for reasons he did not explain, to switch from the conservative majority to the more liberal minority. The change was dramatic for the New Deal and for the future course of the Court. In 1936, the court was still ruling that manufacturing activities conducted within a state did not come under Federal jurisdiction, even though the product manufactured was shipped interstate. "Such effect as they may have upon commerce, however extensive it may be, is secondary and indirect," the Court ruled. One year later, in National Labor Relations Board vs. Jones and Laughlin Steel Corp., Justice Roberts had switched. The traditional view that whatever the steel company did within its home state was not Washington's business was now the minority view. The majority ruled that the NLRB did indeed have the right to get involved. Wrote Justice Hughes: "When industries organize themselves on a national scale, making their relation to interstate commerce the dominant factor in their activities, how can it be maintained that their industrial labor relations constitute a forbidden field into which Congress may not enter when it is necessary to protect interstate commerce from the paralyzing consequences of industrial war? We have often said that interstate commerce itself is a practical conception. It is equally true that interferences with that commerce must be appraised by a judgment that does not ignore actual experience." The Court's tidy distinction between "direct" and "indirect" participation in interstate commerce had long since been recognized as patently ridiculous, as the trend toward concentration created more industries that blanketed the entire nation with their operations and overwhelmed the consumer. The Jones and Laughlin ruling took away from industry one of its few remaining hiding places. It remained only for the Federal government to exercise its powers in the marketplace. The Supreme Court no longer was an obstacle.

The Era of the New Deal took many other steps which recognized the government's responsibility to "promote the general welfare." The Social Security Act, wages and hours laws, and labor laws were all related to industry's reluctance to establish pension plans and its inclination to be insensitive to the health and welfare of its employees. Such "socialist" legislation was bitterly fought as destructive to the very fabric of American Society. In a sense it was; the parts of the fabric woven of *caveat emptor* and *laissez-faire* were ripped away—in principle. A body of laws and institutions had been created in the years since 1900 to regulate competition, to shield the consumer's health, pocketbook, and eardrums. A new theory of the marketplace had been formed.

In practice, however, the effect of this imposing body of law and institutions was meager. In terms of practical accomplishment, of redressing the balance between the buyer and the seller, the history of the consumer movement in the United States up to the 1940's had been a failure. World War II of course had much to do with preventing the consumer from taking advantage of his technical gains. And when the distant battles were fought and won, a nation returning to peace was inevitably more interested in restoring normalcy and prosperity than in rekindling the consumer movement. The economy began to blossom. Thanks to the technological advances spawned by the war, the marketplace grew steadily more complex. One new expression of the electronics age, the TV set, gave industry a powerful new tool to reach its market with advertising, turning that art from an aid to sales into a major industrial enterprise in itself. The marketplace grew more and more concentrated, with the explosive growth of the supermarket, the discount store, and the equally explosive disappearance of the friendly neighborhood storeowner, the last personal link between the producer and the buyer. One lesson of the Depression had been learned, and the age of mass production was joined by the age of mass consumption—which merely meant that the consumer bought more and more goods which he understood less and less. Soap became detergent, rubber became polyethylene, cars became sex symbols. The material existence improved, and the quality of life slowly deteriorated as country-side became housing developments, worms in apples gave way to pesticides, and the air and water grew polluted.

Myriad new ways of taking the decision out of the hands of the consumer were invented. The one-pound box became the 15.6-ounce large economy size. The nickel candy bar went up fifty per cent in size and 100 per cent in price. Advertising discovered the incomplete comparative, and "It's toasted" gave way to "*Luckies* taste better."

The machinery of government, so painstakingly created over half a century, barely creaked along for lack of oil. The FTC, hopelessly swamped by the mere volume of industrial activity around it, tried a few administrative remedies, such as the trade-practice conference, a barely legal device where members of a certain industry got together and decided what was and was not proper. Without any statutory basis for the conferences, the FTC was a most lenient parent to say the least. And its attempts to chase down unfair trade practices were valiant but futile. A Hoover Commission task force reported in 1949: "The Commission has been hampered by inadequate funds, hostile court rulings, mediocre appointments. Its operations, programs, and administrative methods have often been inadequate, and its procedures cumbersome. It has largely become absorbed in petty matters rather than basic problems." The FDA suffered the same lack of money and talent, a deficiency which the best-shaped laws cannot correct. The conscience of Congress could have corrected it, but Congressional consciences were too often directed else-where. In 1953, the FDA ruled that a canner could not take large beets, cut them into little balls, and then label them "baby beets." The chairman of the House Appropriations Committee disagreed most strongly, and cut more than half a million dollars out of the FDA's $5.6-million appropriation as punishment.

Anti-trust legislation never was able to come to grips with the problem of concentration. Size creates all manner of problems in the marketplace, yet no one can say that size *per se* is illegal or even improper. Size makes the American industrial machine go, and nothing will change that even if it should be changed. Improper use of industrial power is illegal—if it is possible to define the word "improper" with anything approaching legal precision, which it seldom is. Now and then, the use of power by a company is so clearly improper that the ill can be remedied. But generally, the anti-trust movement has gotten lost in the shades of gray between the guys in the white and the black hats.

Without consistent support from Congress or from any Administration, without any reliable and realistic leadership of his own, the consumer had little hope of exerting his influence in the marketplace. Virtually anything he wanted was there for the asking, on easy terms, in the showroom or on the storeshelf. All he lacked was the ability to find out exactly what he was buying.

Mutiny in the Marketplace

chapter 4

"...things get very lonely in Washington sometimes. The real voice of the great people of America sometimes sounds faint and distant in that great city."

Woodrow Wilson

S lowly but relentlessly the real voice has been filtering through the once impervious, soundproof walls erected years ago by special interests and buttressed by the Washington bureaucracies where underfinanced regulators dwell. If the consumer is not yet king, his voice is no longer thunderously silent in the legislative and executive counsels of the Capital City. And if the movement is still little more than a randomly organized crusade, an issue-oriented band of aroused consciences whose influence ebbs and flows, the rollcall of legislative triumphs in Congress in the past half-decade serves as a jolting reminder: no matter how awesome may be the forces aligned against social and economic change, they don't win all the big battles anymore. This is not the 1930s or the 1940s or even the early 1960s when consumer dissent was often muffled by the White House and Congress and the regulatory agencies in order to placate the panjandrums of free enterprise. This is a time when the President, as Lyndon Johnson did in 1967, proclaimed to the U.S.: "I don't care how strong the meat lobby is. I want the strongest possible meat inspection bill." Only seven years before, President Eisenhower opposed the Truth-in-Lending bill for fear of ruffling the feathers of GOP businessmen who had long irons into the finance and credit industry.

The rise of a consumer democracy wasn't accomplished quickly. Before the new ambiance was created a few individuals went to prodigious lengths and took some dangerous political risks. Among them: Senators Estes Kefauver, Philip Hart, Gaylord Nelson, Walter Mondale and Warren Magnuson, Representatives Leonor Sullivan, Tom Foley, and Neal Smith, and Rachel Carson, Lyndon B. Johnson, Betty Furness, and Ralph Nader.

The record they have carved is as impressive as the gauntlets they had to run to achieve it. Beginning in 1962 with Estes Kefauver's drug control amendments, the consumer cause gathered momentum, albeit erratic and unsustained. First there was President Kennedy's vigorous consumer message early in the year, proposing a Consumer Bill of Rights. A strong statement by Lyndon Johnson was delivered in 1964, following a lull in 1963, driving home the Kennedy theme. Then, in rising crescendo there poured from Congress between 1966 and 1968 an unparalleled flow of consumer protection legislation, ranging from traffic and tire safety bills to Federal standards on intrastate meat, deceptive credit, radiation hazards, natural gas pipelines and a dozen more. At the same time, Congress launched deep legislative probes into many other areas, from auto insurance to misleading product warranties.

The signal Washington flashed to American industry slowly became clear: regardless of the lobby's strength, if the product or economic service it represents poses a threat to society, or loads the seller's gun at the buyer's expense, no longer can it be insulated from the spotlight of public exposure, legislative action if the industry is unresponsive to change, and administrative vigilance. Health and safety issues could be smothered no more by Washington lawyers.

The legislative response to the existing imbalances between sellers and buyers quite clearly shattered many rules in the politicians' handbook. Historically, nothing has been more unsettling to the average legislator than making a law tinged with controversy, and no bills, with the exception of civil rights in this decade, have been more upsetting than the prospect of a consumer protection bill. A vote against such a bill, after all, could only ring down upon the Congressman the indirect wrath of his silent constituents, the consumers, while a yes vote for a safety bill such as clean meat or safe autos seemed to threaten his very political life. Like ancient clockwork local newspapers would assail him in bitter editorials while local sources of campaign money, such as auto dealers and department stores (upon which the local papers depend), often withdrew their funds.

The U.S. consumer accounts for 70 percent of the spending in the nation's economy, but his lobby has been roughly as potent as a giggling Girl Scout troop in the cloakrooms of Congress where the gut decisions are made. Unhappily for the consumer the forces organized against protection bills, from the Pure Food and Drug Act in 1906 to the Truth-in-Lending bill of 1968, have sailed freely up and down the legislative lagoons, raking with grapeshot the crusaders of change. When legislation was passed it was almost by accident. As political scientist Albert Jay Nock wrote of legislative bodies in general: "They sometimes do a good thing but never because it is a good thing."

Today, when one sniffs the strong scent of consumer-protection sentiment radiating across the nation now that the issues have been found to pack a political wallop, he can readily find abundant evidence that important changes have taken place. The climate for strengthening the hand of the buyer has altered dramatically in a few short years. It has dawned upon politicians and consumers alike that the incredible flood of technical abundance pouring from the country's mills and factories is posing problems to society which the laws and institutions must deal with, as they must with the cancer of urban blight and with the underemployed. What has also changed is that the people who are pointing to the problems are advocates and not reformers. Muckraking anti-business tracts of yesteryear have been replaced in large part by the reasoned pleas of concerned individuals that enlightened selling practices are just as much in the best interests of corporations as they are of the consumer.

And what has changed is that many legislators and some business leaders have come to believe along with Ralph Nader, Betty Furness and Senator Warren Magnuson that only a motley and incomplete patchwork of municipal ordinance, common law product liability, spotty state and Federal law and sporadic voluntary self-regulation currently protects the consumer. The

battle between the ill-equipped consumer and the large institutions is still starkly one-sided, but society no longer automatically
accepts as the price of progress belching smokestacks, cereal-
packed hotdogs, unsafe cars and tires, or deceptive mortgages.
And there are indications that the free enterprise system is no
longer considered by all corporations to be an iron curtain
erected against legislative progress. After all, as E.B.Weiss has
written in *Advertising Age*, "the last 30 years of social advances,
each one fought bitterly by business, has given industry larger and
more consistent profits than in any previous 30 year period."

Now, after two presidents, Kennedy and Johnson, to
varying degrees placed the muscle of their office behind
legislation to put the buyer on a par with the seller, three letters
from private citizens have triggered the callback of 80,000
Mercury Cougars; five letters about unsafe tires resulted in a
hearing, while a phone call from bleary-eyed citizens now sends
the local pollution control board knocking at the door of the
power and light company. A story in the *New Republic* by
Ralph Nader on the sickening state of fish inspection prompted a
crash White House meeting the next day and helped determine the
lines of new legislation. Unprodded, General Motors and Ford
rushed to the market with anti-skid devices and other safety
additions.

"Consumer protection now has sexy political zing," observed auto lobbyist Jerry Sonosky, who fought in many of the
early battles of the decade, first for the Department of Health,
Education, and Welfare during the drug bill and then for Senator
Abraham Ribicoff during the tumultuous auto safety hearings in
1965 and 1966.

A measure of the evolution that has occurred can be found
in Lyndon Johnson's plea for passage of an unprecedented
package of consumer protection legislation in the State of the
Union Message of 1968. To many veterans the theme was
reminiscent of the sentiments only Ralph Nader or a *Consumer
Reports* editorial would have touched two years ago.

The measures, Johnson said, "are a pledge to our people—to
keep them safe in our homes and at work and to give them a fair
deal in the marketplace and I think we must do more. . . .we can
make this truly a new day for the American consumer and by

giving him this protection we can live in history as the consumer-conscious Congress. So let's get on with the work. Let us act soon."

As President Kennedy viewed the scene in 1961, the march of technology had "outmoded many of the old laws and regulations and made new legislation necessary." That technology was affecting "the foods we eat, medicines we take and the many appliances we use in our homes."

The late President was also concerned about the lack of proper consumer information in the marketplace. The consumer's choice, he said, "is influenced by mass advertising utilizing highly developed arts of persuasion. The consumer typically cannot know whether drug preparations meet minimum standards of safety, quality and efficacy. He usually does not know how much he pays for consumer credit; whether one prepared food has more nutritional value than another; whether the performance of a product will in fact meet his needs; or whether the 'large economy size' is really a bargain."

In his message Kennedy proposed that the American consumer should be armed with four basic rights:

1) The right to safety—to be protected against the marketing of goods which are hazardous to health or life.

2) The right to be informed—to be protected against fraudulent, deceitful or grossly misleading information, advertising labeling or other practices and to be given the facts he needs to make an informed choice.

3) The right to choose—to be assured access wherever possible to a variety of products and services at competitive prices, and in those industries in which competition is not workable and government regulation is substituted as an assurance of satisfactory quality at fair prices.

4) The right to be heard—to be assured that consumer interest will receive full and sympathetic consideration in the formulation of government policy and fair, expeditious treatment in administration tribunals.

Kennedy was sincere in his views (though he was never as tangibly committed to the consumer as Johnson later became), but his relations with Congress were erratic at best and no significant roadblocks were hurdled during his brief days in office. Other issues had to take priority. Nevertheless, Kennedy's

theme received some outside reinforcement in 1962. The eyes of
politicians and businessmen were suddenly opened by the late
Rachel Carson's shocking account in *Silent Spring* of man's
senseless assault on the environment and the horrifying industrial
contamination of air, soil, rivers and oceans. She wrote that
"future historians may well be amazed by our distorted sense of
proportion," and detailed the environmental impact of endless
gallons of chemicals pouring almost unchecked from laboratories,
non-selective chemicals with the power to enter living organisms
after being sprayed on crops and soils, passing "from one to
another in a chain of poisoning and death. Or they pass
mysteriously by underground streams until they emerge and
through the alchemy of air and sunlight, combine into new forms
that kill vegetation, sicken cattle and work unknown harm on
those who drink from once pure wells." And she told of new
aerosols, dusts and sprays which killed good insects and bad and
possessed the power to "still the song of birds and the leaping of
fish in the streams, to coat the leaves with a deadly film and to
linger on in the soil."

Who was responsible? Was it possible that the cream of
American business whose soothing advertisements invaded
millions of American living rooms via television was poisoning
the environment?

Many readers agreed with Miss Carson's analysis of the
problem: "It is the public that is being asked to assume the
risks. . . .the public must decide whether it wishes to continue on
the present road and it can do so only when in full possession of
the facts. In the words of Jean Rostand, 'the obligation to endure
gives us the right to know'."

The tenets of the new consumerism had never been put
forth more powerfully than in Miss Carson's book, and her
concern for conservation of natural resources and her bitter anger
at industry's lack of priorities, when fused with the late President
Kennedy's pleas for restoration of quality to American life and
LBJ's populism, formed the political underpinnings for the out-
burst of legislative activity that followed in 1966-68.

Yet the consumer protection movement during the first
half of the 1960s was for the most part limited and sporadic,
though not because the White House wasn't aware of the plight of
the buyer. On Capitol Hill, most legislators still had to be shown

that consumers needed protection. The prevailing view in industry was also the majority view in the Senate and House. In the words of General Foods Chairman Charles Mortimer, "the free enterprise system is the consumer's best protector." To think otherwise was not just heretical but dangerous.

Senator Estes Kefauver's fight for drug industry regulation was a classic example of what happens when a legislator raises his voice above the noisy countervailing forces of Big Government and Big Business and is assailed by them. James Madison in the Federalist Papers aptly described what motivates such forces against change:

"They are actuated by some common impulse of passion, or of interest, adverse to the right of other citizens or to the permanent and aggregate interests of the community."

These forces are oblivious, at first, even to unassailable evidence that their passions are misdirected. Kefauver, for example, had mountains of documented evidence that some drug companies were ringing up 5000 per cent profit on certain drugs despite the unalterable fact that many of them were either worthless or dangerous. Kefauver battled and bullied his congressional peers and eventually, a year before he died, got most of his legislation passed. He succeeded in spite of widespread public apathy, lack of White House interest and merciless opposition from the drug industry and its congressional supporters. An unequal contest? The drug industry and the Pharmaceutical Manufacturers Association spent at least $5 million in the abortive attempt to discredit both Kefauver and the bill while the Tennessee Senator had at most $300,000 in resources during the four-year battle. Only at the end when it sensed the rising level of public outrage did the industry conclude that some face saving legislation was probably needed. The industry's legislative strategists correctly figured that far too many people had read of the hearings and of drug executives' opposition to even the flimsiest preventative measures against overpriced and dangerous drugs.

Contributing to the outrage was testimony of the sort delivered by Dr. Dale Console, former Medical Director of Squibb. At one point during the hearings the dialogue centered on the drug industry's contention that high research costs justified high prices because not all research efforts succeeded.

"This is true," Console told the committee, "since it is the very essence of research. The problem arises out of the fact that they market so many of their failures."

Kefauver then asked him if, in his opinion, much of the industry's research led to the marketing of drugs that were useless or worse.

"I think more than half is in that category," Dr. Console answered. "And I should point out that with many of these products it is clear that while they are on the drawing board that they promise no utility. They promise sales."

A horrified pill-taking public learned from similar statements and from the thalidomide revelations that drug-makers and doctors were not infallible, that present laws were lax and that the stream of new pill compounds flooding the market at the rate of six a week was not necessarily made up of wonder drugs. And they heard, many for the first time, that a doctor could legally give a patient an unapproved new drug as part of widespread clinical testing without advising the patient that the drug was experimental. They also learned that the Food and Drug Administration had budget enough for only 24 full-time people to hold back the flood of questionable drugs.

In the end, Kefauver won, but considering the lengths to which the industry went to squelch the bill, the final amendments seem rather benign. It was, however, a beginning. Automatic approval of new drugs was abolished, proof of efficacy was required for old and new drugs, and when cases of false and misleading advertising were established, the products would henceforth be ordered withdrawn. Before the bill was finally passed and signed in August 1962, Kefauver had to weather a vicious personal attack by the drug industry imputing to him leftwing leanings, and only lukewarm White House support.

What he was fighting, in the end, were the philosophical descendants of those who had similarly tried to dismember the Pure Food and Drug Act of 1906 and the 1938 amendments, all passed, as Kefauver's were, after public outrage had crystallized. Unquestionably the thalidomide revelations in 1962 gave impetus to Kefauver's efforts as the Elixir Sulfanilamide deaths had to legislation in the 1930s.

In all instances the drug industry's strategy was inflexibly similar. Publicly, one industry chieftain after another proclaimed everlasting belief in strong food and drug laws while quietly lining up the best lawyers in Washington to assure that no laws were passed.

The more things change, the more they remain the same. Dr. Robert Fischelis wrote an editorial in 1938 for the *New Jersey Journal of Pharmacy*, the substance of which was as bitingly appropriate during the 1962 drug hearings as it was when he wrote it on the heels of the elixir deaths. Called "Have They Died in Vain," the editorial in part stated that the "medical profession has been entirely too ready to rely upon the advertising claims of drug products without requiring scientific proof of therapeutic value and safety. The drug manufacturing industry has been entirely too eager to produce products for profit without due regard for the hazards involved in combining drugs without complete knowledge of the effect of such combinations... lawmakers have been entirely too ready to listen to and act upon the arguments of constituents with a personal interest in the emasculation of laws and regulations which provide the kind of control that is in the best interests of the public...let the industry now show whether it is dominated by dollars or by some conception of the responsibility that goes with the production of agents directly affecting human lives.

"It is not sufficient to say 'we believe in strong food and drug laws' and offer amendments designed to weaken governmental control over the very things that close the door to fraud and quackery."

Just after the Senate roll call on the Kefauver bill, which passed 78 - 0 when opponents jumped on the public safety bandwagon, Senator Paul Douglas took the floor and said: "The American people will be eternally grateful to Estes Kefauver.... Can we learn from this lesson or can mankind educate himself only by disaster and tragedy?"

But the accomplishments of Kefauver, the gangly hillbilly with the whip-smart brain, were never fully appreciated at the time. And the forces he had unleashed, exposing the social costs of the profit motive, diffused again. However, they didn't remain that way for long.

In 1964, Lyndon Johnson detected the winds of change and issued a strong Consumer Message, calling for twelve new laws, from truth-in-lending to stiff control of pesticides, from

meat inspection to more drug inspection. No response came from
Capitol Hill. But as an indication of the priorities he placed on
the issue, in January Johnson did appoint Mrs. Esther Peterson to
the new White House post of Special Assistant for Consumer
Affairs. Meantime, in the absence of new congressional action,
the Federal Trade Commission halted a record number of
unlawful business practices. It was also the year when for the
fifth straight time the Senate Banking and Currency Committee
failed to report out Senator Paul Douglas' truth-in-lending bill,
partly because of Chairman Willis Robertson's contention that
stating interest charges at simple annual rates would cause
economic dislocations in the credit industry.

In 1965, Johnson skipped a Consumer Message. No one
knows for certain why he did, but some congressional observers
felt he didn't convey a sense of urgency in the area for fear of
provoking hostility among major industries. In the absence of
White House proclamations, however, there were the first
glimmerings of the new era, still a full two years away.

Although a wide variety of proposals for the creation of
special councils and study groups on consumer interests never
even cleared committee in either chamber that year, and
truth-in-lending was buried again, Congress did step into the drug
area and gave the Food and Drug Administration stronger controls
over the illegal sale of barbiturates, amphetamines and counterfeit
drugs.

The cigarette controversy also jumped into the headlines
when a mild labeling bill, calling for packages to be stamped with
a health warning, was passed, overruling a stiffer Federal Trade
Commission recommendation of the previous year. It was the
Congress' response to the Surgeon General's report in 1964 which
concluded that "smoking was a health hazard of sufficient
importance in the U. S. to warrant appropriate remedial action."

When the issue was debated in the Senate and House,
opposition in many other industries to government encroachment
on business practices jelled. The political pressure put on the
legislators and, some contend, on the White House, was such that
the 1964 Federal Trade Commission rule requiring that all
cigarette advertising contain the health warning did not receive a
personal endorsement from Lyndon Johnson, as truth-in-
packaging and truth-in-lending had, and the tobacco industry

succeeded in obtaining the far softer bill. The lobbying techniques, forged by former Kentucky Congressmen Earle Clements
(he was Senate Democratic Whip under LBJ during the 1953-56
sessions) were directed at de-emphasizing the possible connection
between cigarettes and health and, instead, winning Congressmen
over to the view that the proposed FTC rules posed grave
"economic and idealogical dangers." The FTC lost and was
prohibited from pursuing its across-the-board advertising warning
for five years, until 1969.

The White House was thrown for a loss on its proposed bill
to control pesticides and settled for a bill increasing the
authorization for pesticide research funds. LBJ's bill would have
forced manufacturers to open their factories to inspection,
"clearly placing the burden of proof of safety on the proponent
of the chemical rather than on the government." Some congressional sources believe that interagency bickering over the bill's
wording and poorly timed introduction killed all chances from
the start.

While most of the consumer bills were dying, the seeds of
future victories were being sewn in the auto safety field which
had first been probed by Congressman Kenneth Roberts of
Alabama in the mid-1950s. In the course of questioning whether
Detroit was designing cars with safety in mind, Roberts learned
that energy and perserverance in the absence of strong support
was ineffective. Before the hearings had proceeded very far he
was drowned in a flood of hostility from the industry and
opposition from government agencies supposedly in charge of
safety. Even more damaging to his quest was the apathy of his
own peers on Capitol Hill. Though the hearings didn't produce
remedial legislation, the Pandora's Box was opened slightly. A
forum was made available for points of view other than the jaded
defense of Detroit that it "had its shoulder to the safety wheel."
Independent engineers gave their views, as did crash injury
specialists and physicians. As an industry executive conceded
recently: "That was the beginning of the end for the argument
that the only problems with autos were drunks and nuts behind
the wheel."

In 1965, as an administrative action, the General Services
Administration published a list of 17 auto safety devices to be
made mandatory on new cars purchased from Detroit by the

government. The safety additions included seat belts, padded dashboards, impact-absorbing steering columns and recessed steering wheels. On April 1, Senator Gaylord Nelson, after warning that "tire manufacturing and marketing industries today contain the seeds of national scandal," introduced a bill authorizing the Commerce Department to require tire producers to follow specified safety and performance standards. The hullabaloo which ensued was deafening as auto industry lobbyists fought to avoid the safety issue. They couldn't. Nelson insisted during hearings that "no accurate information" on tire safety existed and the consumer had no "way of appraising hazy and contradictory information." His case was supported by the testimony of Allan Bratman, then president of the Market Tire Company, who charged that "tire marketing represents a pattern of abuses which is unparalleled" and insisted that minimum safety standards alone "will not terminate deception in the retail marketing of tires."

The Senate Commerce Committee then heard tire industry representatives reject that argument. A sample of the widespread attitude is found in the words of Winston Marsh, then executive vice president of the National Tire Dealers and Retailers Association: "Grade labeling would be an impairment to free enterprise."

Rubber Manufacturers Association President Ross Ormsby escalated the counterattack. State tire inspection laws were the answer, Ormsby stated, "because an oversimplified system of grading and labeling would. . .encourage manufacturers to conform closely to established grades by eliminating product differences," and would thereby "rob the consumer of his wide range of choice and would tend to stultify the industry's initiative in research and its spirit of innovation and product improvement which have brought tires to their present level of safe, dependable service for every type of need and for every pocketbook."

A testament to the tire industry's spirit and service was then delivered by General Services Administration commissioner Heinz Abersfeller: "Under current conditions the consumer has no idea what he is buying."

That spring congressional investigators unearthed facts which established the degree to which tire production was dominated by the auto industry. The thrust was simply that the incentive to reduce unit costs that the auto companies drilled home to Goodyear and Goodrich "discourages both the production and the purchase of really high quality tires which many motorists should be using." Those are the words of Senator Nelson, who six weeks before calling for the Tire Act had introduced a bill asking the General Services Administration to set safety standards on all autos sold in interstate commerce. In June Connecticut Senator Ribicoff offered a traffic safety research plan.

The pressure was building. In addition to the promulgation of safety standards on government cars, New York had established an auto safety board with authority to construct a prototype safe car; the Illinois House of Representatives passed a bill requiring the GSA standards for all state-owned cars, and Maryland decided to require tire safety standards.

In mid-July of 1965, Senator Ribicoff convened another round of hearings on traffic safety. "Public interest in. . .safety is at a new all-time peak," he said. "It is apparent that we have little if any national policy regarding traffic safety—especially as it relates to the private automobile. All other forms of passenger-carrying vehicles must satisfy certain Federal safety requirements, except the private auto. It is absurd and tragic when you consider that special messages calling for the expenditure of billions of dollars are sent to Congress to fight the three leading causes of death—heart attack, cancer, and stroke—but a report on the fourth leading cause of death—traffic deaths—still has not been made public."

If public interest was rising, it was not plainly evident to the top executives of Ford, General Motors, Chrysler and American Motors, as witnessed by their replies to Ribicoff's probes during the hearings. General Motors board chairman Frederick Donner, for one, told the committee that installment of safety features depended to a large extent on public acceptance: "If we were to force on people things they are not prepared to buy, we would face a consumer revolt. . .for these reasons the improvement of our automobiles—in safety as well as in other areas—has been evolutionary." A few stomachs turned at that statement of corporate quibbling, but not many. A few more choked in disbelief when GM President James Roche said he had reservations about the "economic advisability" of a mandatory smog control system on all cars on a national basis since it had not been proven that such a system was needed in many areas of the country.

Roche stated further that safer cars alone could "not be viewed as a panacea for the highway safety problem. . .state and local governments have the major responsibility of this area."

An angry Senator, the late Robert Kennedy of New York, challenged General Motors. Did they know of a Cornell University study indicating that GM doors were more prone to flying off during a collision than the doors of other makes? GM didn't. Kennedy was horrified that a company which was racking up a $1.7 billion net profit annually not only was pushing responsibility off on the states, but had neither the finances nor the inclination to improve safety.

Representing the Chrysler Corporation was Harry Chesebrough. His remedy: the government should establish and finance a center to study the cause of traffic accidents. Amazed at this stalling tactic, Ribicoff asked the Chrysler witness about a rash of 1965 Dodges, Plymouth and Chryslers that had been sold with steering mechanisms that could break away from their moorings unless rewelded. Chrysler knew about the situation, Chesebrough admitted, and had notified dealers. The owners were never told.

"I am shocked," Senator Kennedy shouted. By that time he wasn't alone.

Finally, the statement that virtually assured that a messy confrontation was inevitable was provided by American Motors President Roy Abernathy. His neat assessment: it's not a question of the car at all, since "all indications point to driver attitude as the most significant factor in accidents." Besides, he told the Senators, existing laws were adequate.

The only voice of enlightenment that day was that of Ford President Arjay Miller (as it was to be again in 1968). He didn't make himself the most popular man at the Bloomfield Hills Country Club bar after he conceded that "safety sells cars." The industry had to do more than it was doing, he asserted, and he reinforced Ford's support by doubling the company's financial commitment to safety.

The hearings concluded with attention still focused on the driver and not on the safety of cars or the quality control of auto production. The auto industry had won again. Or had it? Just two months after Ribicoff's hearings ended, Lyndon Johnson made a speech which clearly paved the way for a reappraisal of U. S. industry's policies toward the consumer and the year ended on a note of hope for consumerists.

". . .the time has come," he said, "to bury forever the myth that furthering the interest of the consumer must be at the expense of the producer. There is, I am convinced, a common interest between Americans and their capacity as producers and in their capacity as consumers. This mutuality must be emphasized." The tide was slowly turning.

Even as the President spoke a printing press was grinding out a book by an unknown Harvard law graduate named Ralph Nader. It was called *Unsafe at Any Speed.** The repercussions of the book, the ensuing investigation of Nader by General Motors and the swift passage of a powerful Federal Law the next summer added up to one conclusion: the third consumer revolution of the 20th century had begun.

*Grossman Publishers, Inc., N.Y., N.Y., 1965.

The New Muckrakers

chapter 5

If Ralph Nader suddenly pulled up stakes tomorrow, abandoning the consumer battlefields of Washington for a comfortable corporate law practice, he would nevertheless have earned an unchallenged niche in the history of the decade. He has raised new issues, and added new dimensions to the lobbyist's traditional role while driving dramatically home the message that consumer protection means something more than folksy shopping hints in the local suburban newspaper.

For four years Nader has raced up and down the halls of Congress and into the regulatory catacombs, alerting legislators and government officials to the inequities and imbalances extant in the economy, whether they be exploding gas pipelines, hazardous television sets or rotten hamburgers. His battle cry: nothing more or less than the qualitative reform of the industrial revolution is at stake.

One of the first men to meet Nader when he arrived in Washington from Connecticut in 1964 was one of Senator Ribicoff's staff aides, Philip Cook, now Rome Bureau Chief for *Newsweek*.

"With his ragged tweed overcoat, his tie all askew, and his long bony hands shooting out of a worn, rumpled suit," Cook recalls, "Nader was like a dozen other kooky inventors who constantly turned up to pester us with a safety idea that would save millions of lives. Like the others, he was inflamed over the monstrous indifference of Detroit. But unlike the others, he'd been around; he was no dreamer or romantic. He had a lawyer's mind and he came armed with the facts. We discovered quickly that he knew more than most people at Ford or General Motors about the auto industry. He had a network of spies throughout the industry, faceless people in the engineering departments who didn't have the guts to resign in protest over the shoddy work they saw around them but who would spill their guts to Nader over a cup of coffee.

"He was a congressional staffer's dream. He had all the data and the names and phone numbers of people who could substantiate everything he said. For some of us, he was too good to be true."

In issue after issue the self-appointed consumer lobbyist has proved himself a remarkably effective political and economic force, opposing the centers of power he believes frequently infringe on the rights of the individual: Business, Government and Labor. This contemporary David not only lobbies for consumer bills, but he serves Congressmen and cabinet members as a witness, investigator, freelance speechwriter and strategist. Though his enemies consider him a publicity seeker, Nader's methods refute the charge. "If I can get three Senators to say something," he explained early in 1968, "that's better than for me to say it. I don't need more enemies. Sometimes it's more effective for me to stay on the sidelines."

Why would such a young, intelligent man choose such a lonely life? His childhood years in Connecticut provide one key, but his experiences at Princeton and Harvard probably determined the final choice.

Winsted is an old New England mill town tucked away in the foothills of the Berkshire mountains in northwestern Connecticut. From afar the 200-year-old hamlet is a Christmas-card montage of small shuttered white wooden houses and proud church steeples set against the sky. But the view from Main Street is less picturesque. On the far side of the street stands a clutter of graceless two-story wood and brick buildings housing Town Hall, the fire department and the Highland Arms Restaurant. Once there was a scattering of small, red brick factories across the street along the Mad River, but a flood washed them away years ago. It was here that Nader was born on February 27, 1934, the son of Lebanese parents, Nathra and Rose who had migrated to Winsted nine years before and opened the Highland Arms.

Older residents among the Italian, Polish and Yankee population remember Ralph as a reserved boy who loved books, Joe Dimaggio and first base. From the start his father exerted a powerful influence; business problems were never too pressing to prevent the family from holding long and heated discussions about national and local politics or any current issue. From these discussions emerged a prediction from Nathra. Ralph would be the lawyer of the family.

"The Naders are dreamers," remembers 82-year-old Mrs. Isabelle Pearson, who taught all four of the Nader children— Shaffeak, Claire, Laura, and Ralph—during her 43 years at the local high school now named for her.

"They are Lebanese you know," she says. "They dream dreams and have visions. I think that if they had an idea for any project they were interested in, they wouldn't consider the possibility that it couldn't be done. The underdog has always appealed to that family."

The Nader family has always made itself heard in Winsted. Nathra, 73, who still helps run the restaurant, long ago developed the reputation of a spokesman for change and social justice at town meetings where he organized programs to lure new business when the mills began to shut down. "If you are going to build a nation," he told his children, "you have to get up on your feet and speak out."

Nathra's stout stands against the forces of status quo in conservative Winsted are remembered well, if not always fondly, by some of the older Yankee residents as is his deep, consuming belief in the efficacy of the American dream. From the first all the children were instilled with a strong sense of social responsibility; Nathra had the poignant simplicity of an immigrant who cherished his adopted land.

"We made Ralph understand that working for justice in this country is a safeguard of our democracy," he told a visitor a few months ago.

Laura Nader Milleron, one of Ralph's two older sisters, remembers that her father would tell them, "you should give twice as much back to society as you take. Things at home were always more stimulating than they are here at the University."

An associate professor of Anthropology at Berkeley, Mrs. Milleron believes that Ralph has drawn deeply from his childhood for his crusades. "He developed a wonderful objectivity about the world about him. He has learned to stand away from things and analyze with his beautiful mind the world around him. It's something you grow up with. Nothing that he has done since he left Winsted has surprised us."

Ralph made an impressive record at high school as a first baseman and as a scholar. He graduated with honors, exhibiting a flair for languages. Already fluent in Arabic and English, he was soon to master Russian, Chinese, Spanish and Portugese.

When the rangy 17-year-old with jet-black hair and flashing brown eyes went off to Princeton in the fall of 1951, his father's many wise words went with him: "No person is bigger than you are and no one is any smaller. Don't ever look up or look down on anyone, either."

Princeton was a stimulating but confusing experience for young Nader; the sense of dignified indignation he inherited from his father found reinforcement along the tree-shaded paths and in the classrooms. What struck him was the lemming-like conformity of most of the students. He registered his opposition to the herd instinct by refusing to wear white buckskin shoes, the *sine qua non* of a Princeton man in those days. And when he found the curriculum too rigid for his needs he chose the most flexible, unfashionable major: Oriental studies.

His first collision with the arbitrary use of power occurred after he noticed flocks of dead birds scattered under the bushes lining the paths. A brief inquiry revealed evidence that heavy doses of DDT had killed them. He was outraged. When the editor of the university paper received a letter from Nader complaining of the carnage, he discarded it. "It was unbelievable," he recalled long afterwards, "not only did the editor fail to print my letter but he didn't even see what the issue was."

Nader made similar progress with the campus authorities about the lack of proper appeal machinery for expelled students. Indifference and blank stares greeted his attempts to ignite the passions of his classmates.

Nader worked hard enough in between these sociological escapades to earn a *magna cum laude* degree in 1955. Sometimes he worked too hard. Once the campus police caught him lowering himself through a basement at the Woodrow Wilson school after hours because he needed some special research for a project. He landed on top of one of his professors who was sitting on the john under the window. "After that," a friend recalled, "they made Ralph a special key."

It was at Harvard Law School the following fall that he happened upon the issue that eventually catapulted him into the national spotlight: automobile safety. As he read one case history after another his curiosity increased; trips to the engineering department at M.I.T. nearby confirmed some of his initial impressions. The law unfairly placed emphasis in accident cases on the driver and virtually none on the engineering and design faults of the car. Frustration mushroomed into anger after several of his friends were killed or severely injured. By then he had gathered impressive evidence, he thought, which added up to a general conclusion: Detroit's manufacturers not only were oblivious to safety but resisted all outside pressures for reform.

As Nader saw it, though the industry was abundantly endowed with man's genius to provide an engineering environment for both highway and car which could better protect drivers from, in Nader's words, "the consequences of their errors," it was holding back the tide of innovation, change and evolution, free from sanction for their misdirected priorities: placing styling and horsepower over safety.

When he sought out students at Harvard Law, hoping to find others who shared his outraged disbelief, he found himself wallowing in the same intellectual mire he had been in at Princeton. No one seemed to care about the gap between what was possible in car manufacturing and what was actual, given the tremendous advances in science and engineering during the post war years.

As he later related to a Congressional committee, "I became incensed at the way there can be a tremendous amount of injustice and brutality in an industrialized society without any accountability, without any responsibility; that people sitting in executive suites can make remote decisions which will someday result in carnage, and because they are remote in time and space between their decision and the consequences of that decision, there is no accountability."

What started with concern over the sorry state of auto safety rapidly escalated for Nader into doubts about the adequacy of the corporate institution to perform in the public interest. Were corporations working in the consumer's interest or were they consumed by the need to increase profits at all costs? Did avenues for corporate reform exist? Was it possible to infuse both corporations and Washington regulatory agencies with an awareness of the social costs of unbridled, mass production?

Such questions gnawed at him during his years at Harvard Law, an institution he terms a "highpriced tool factory," and while serving a six month Army hitch at Fort Dix in 1959. Soon afterward, during the early months of private law practice in Hartford, Connecticut in 1960, the first tenets of his safety and reform crusade hardened into shape. It seemed to him that corporate irresponsibility was not confined to the shabby fly-by-night hucksters skittering around on the fringes of an otherwise flawless, healthy, free enterprise system, as leading businessmen had always argued. What of the fact, as the Food and Drug Administration and Congress were beginning to establish, that many drug companies, including giants such as Merck and Smith, Kline and French, had deliberately falsified test results on new drugs so that the FDA would approve them for sale sooner?

And what about the downright refusal of the major auto companies to notify owners that the cars they were driving were defective?

If chicanery and malfeasance were confined solely to door-to-door salesmen, peddling worthless, sometimes dangerous merchandise, why was it that the Greyhound Bus company used regrooved tires on most high-speed turnpike runs? A Federal investigator, examining the details of several fatal accidents later confirmed Nader's allegations. The causes were defective tires.

Before long, Ralph Nader was a very outraged young man. While negligent drivers, embezzlers or robbers drew increasingly stiff jail terms, large corporations which allowed defective products to be marketed had, with the help of legions of lawyers, insulated and immunized themselves against comparable penalties. Culpable executives almost always went untouched.

Where did the responsibility rest for products that killed 60,000 people a year in non-auto accidents and maimed at least 9 million more? Was the price of progress the startling finding of a Consumers Union study that 376 brand-name, heavily advertised appliances and television sets were unacceptable for household use because of the dangers they posed?

In those early Hartford years, however, Nader's central concern was with auto safety. He roamed up and down the state, sometimes hitchhiking to lecture dates before civic groups in his effort to rally forces of reform.

"The true mark of a humane society," he told one local gathering, "must be what it does about the prevention of accident injuries, not the cleaning up of them afterward."

But wherever he wandered there was strong opposition to his message; either that or blank stares. He didn't stop. To another group, he said, "the gigantic costs of highway carnage in this country support a service industry. A vast array of services—medical, police, administrative, legal, insurance, automotive repair and funeral—stand equipped to handle the direct and indirect consequences of accident injuries." Besides the human losses, Nader calculated that highway accidents cost $8.3 billion annually in property damage, medical expenses and insurance. "But these are not the kind of costs which fall on the builders of motor vehicles," he wrote in *Unsafe at Any Speed* in 1965. "Except for a few successful law suits for negligent construction of the vehicle the proper foot is not pinched. Instead the costs fall to the users of the vehicles, who are in no position to dictate safer automobile designs."

In early 1964, convinced by then of the utter futility of battling on the state and local level he carried his mini-crusade to Washington. Recalling that a Massachusetts legislator had once thundered at him to get out of the state and go back to Hartford, Nader later mused: "I learned that General Motors was bigger than those two states. I had watched years go by without reform; before that decades had gone by. Maybe in Washington I'd find out whether General Motors was bigger than the U.S. government, too."

Nearly penniless, Nader arrived in the Capitol, and landed several consulting jobs for Senate committees. His main task for the next 12 months, however, was to develop a position paper for Assistant Secretary of Labor Daniel Moynihan, spelling out what government policy should be toward auto safety.

Even then there were forces converging that would soon make consumer protection on incendiary political issue. Senators

Ribicoff and Nelson revealed plans to hold investigative hearings into auto and tire safety, sensing a more liberal climate in Congress after the 1964 Democratic landslide.

In the nation's courts there were similar signs that the times would soon change. In several key cases the burden of liability for defective autos showed a slight shift to the manufacturer, a legal trend that later picked up a billowing head of steam.

In *Henningsen v. Bloomfield Motors*, a landmark case, a new economic and social concept in warranty law was expressed by a New Jersey state court. "We see no rational doctrinal basis," the court wrote, "for differentiating between a fly in a bottle of beverage and a defective automobile. . .Accordingly we hold that when a manufacturer puts a new automobile into a stream of trade and promotes its purchase by the public, an implied warranty that it is reasonably suitable for use as such accompanies it into the hands of the ultimate purchaser."

Though the slow erosion of the ancient concept of *caveat emptor* was accelerated by Henningsen and similar cases, most legislators were still far from ready to accept Nader's promise that something was amiss on the production lines of Detroit. The prevailing view in Congress and among state legislators was that the auto industry was above reproach and under no circumstances vulnerable to a charge that top auto officials were insensitive to danger or, when quality control broke down, sold unsafe cars.

Nader finished his job for Moynihan, and armed with a mountain of data and engineering studies gleaned from his network of private, faceless sources, holed up in a tiny $80-a-month apartment in downtown Washington to put together the grisly safety record of America's largest industry in *Unsafe at Any Speed*. When he wasn't writing, he was feeding ideas and leads to congressional committee aides or pressing regulatory agency men to open their eyes and look at the world. To say the least, the regulatory climate Nader perceived was quiescent, save for the new frontiers in investor protection being explored by Securities and Exchange Commission Chairman Manuel Cohen. Nader concurred completely with an assessment of that climate by Lee Loevinger, assistant attorney general for Antitrust under Kennedy and a Federal Communications Commission member under Lyndon Johnson:

Unfortunately, the history of every regulatory agency in the government is that it comes to represent the industry or groups it's supposed to control. All of these agencies were fine when they were first set up, but before long they became infiltrated by the regulatees and are now more or less run by and for them. It's not a question of venality either. More, the agency people consort with this or that representative of some special interest-group and finally they all come to think alike. Every company that's concerned about government control and is big enough to manage hires a man—maybe four or five men—at anywhere from thirty to seventy thousand dollars a year to find out what we're up to. And by God, they find out. They wine and dine agency people and get to be great friends with them. Like a lot of people without much money, some bureaucrats are impressed by being around big shots and by the big life. Sooner or later, all of these agencies end up with constituents. And they represent them damn well, too.

Lobbyists, Congressmen and regulators watched Nader closely, looking for weaknesses. His one-man style annoyed some; his pledge to stake out an area in which there was no compromise struck others as the words of an idealistic crackpot. He didn't fit any familiar Washington pattern. A Senate aide came close with this characterization: "Ralph is a basically sound fanatic."

When *Unsafe* was published in the fall of 1965, none of the mystery diminished. It increased. But, nearly overnight, thousands of car owners were poking one another in disbelief. In detailed, crisp fashion, Nader described the designed-in dangers of the U.S. car. He cast the industry in the role of the villain for placing styling and sales over safety. It was a strong recipe for controversy. The regrettable situation existed, wrote Nader, because no economic incentive was present for the companies to install safety features, such as collapsible steering columns and buttressed doors, since the costs and penalties were borne for the most part by the driver, not the manufacturer. Whereas drivers would always be prone to error, much remained to be done to make cars themselves safer, particularly to protect the driver from a second collision with the car interior. Anything was worth trying, he pleaded, if it reduced the fantastic highway death rate even slightly.

"A principal reason why the automobile has remained the only transportation vehicle to escape being called to a meaningful public account," Nader wrote, "is that the public never has been supplied the information nor offered the quality of competition to enable it to make effective demands through the marketplace and through government for safe, nonpolluting and efficient automobiles that can be produced economically."

He even quoted Sir Francis Bacon to underscore his cry for reform: ". . .He that will not apply new remedies must expect new evils, for time is the greatest innovator."

Nader served up one hair-raising tale after another in the best-selling book, but none moreso than the case of Mrs. Rose Pierini. While driving just beyond the San Marcos overpass on Hollister Street in Santa Barbara, California in 1961, her *Chevrolet Corvair* unaccountably turned over and crashed, severing her left arm. Highway patrol officers discovered that the left tire had been punctured by the wheel rim, indicating that the rear engine car had a serious stability problem. Mrs. Pierini was absolved. At a trial later, Officer Charles Hanna testified that he had "had many chances to observe accidents involving this type of vehicle" and referred to a confidential circular put out to officers by the Highway Patrol detailing the handling hazards of certain rear-engine cars, mainly the General Motors Corvair. "They all have the same type of pattern," he said.

The court heard service manager James Johnson of the Washburn Chevrolet agency, where the car was bought, relate that he had visited the General Motors training center. There he was told, he testified, that differential tire pressures, front and rear, in *Corvairs* were a critical factor in their stability. There followed this exchange.

> *Counsel:* Were you instructed by your superiors to tell members of the public that tire pressures on the *Corvair* were vital, important, crucial and critical?
>
> *Johnson:* No.
>
> *Counsel:* Did you instruct your subordinates to tell members of the public and customers of Washburn Chevrolet that tire pressures on the *Corvair* were vital, important, crucial or critical?
>
> *Johnson:* We didn't tell the public this, no.
>
> *Counsel:* Is it true that tire pressures on a *Corvair* are a must; they have got to be just right for the stability of the car?
>
> *Johnson:* Yes.

Further indications as to how General Motors alerted
its dealers were provided when owner Washburn was questioned.

Counsel: When did you first learn that you were to sell
Corvair automobiles?

Washburn: Oh, it was sometime during the year 1959. I
don't recall the exact month.

Counsel: Did General Motors or the Chevrolet division advise
you about the engineering of the *Corvair* at any time before
you started selling that car to the public?

Washburn: The only things I had seen from Chevrolet
Motors Division was what we call sales training films which
we use, before we have a new car announcement, to train
our salesmen. And they had films on the *Corvair* in it, in
this kit which we get every year to train salesmen on the
new product.

Counsel: But there was nothing in the films you saw about
the engineering of the *Corvair*, was there?
Washburn: No.

Counsel: The Chevrolet division shipped those cars, those
Corvairs, to you without giving you any information about
the engineering; correct?

Washburn: That is correct.

Counsel: And you started selling those to the public without having any engineering information of the car, true?

Washburn: Yes, yes; well, with the exception of this one
school that Mr. Johnson attended.

Testimony also produced the fact that General Motors
provided dealers with regular production option 696, which they
could sell to *Corvair* owners. RPO 696 included heavier suspen-
sion springs, larger shock absorbers, a front stabilizer bar and
rear-axle rebound straps to reduce excessive caving in or
"tuck-under" of the rear wheels on cornering or other stress
situations. This option was factory installed and not openly
advertised. Mrs. Pierini hadn't known about the option. General
Motors, rather than let the trial produce more revelations settled
out of court for $70,000. By October 1965, more than one
hundred suits alleging instability in the *Corvair* had been filed
around the country. G.M. tried to place the onus on driver
negligence but they lost many cases.

Nader's account of the Pierini case, and his systematic exposure of Detroit's upside-down safety priorities, was dynamite. Mandatory standards were needed to remedy the situation, Nader concluded. Besides earning himself some much-needed pocket money (the book has sold 60,000 hardback copies, 400,000 paperback) Nader's book altered the congressional climate for a safety bill, but more obstacles still had to be hurdled first.

The Bill

Until 1966, the automobile industry enjoyed a unique position in the U.S. transportation system; unlike airlines, railroads and trucks, it was virtually free from federal regulation, a situation that produced in the corporate headquarters' thousands of miles away little inclination to establish strong, durable communications links with Congressmen and administration officials.

The year before Senator Ribicoff had steered his hearings to the brink of a confrontation. That should have been a warning to the industry, company men have since conceded privately, but the top men still believed that the excitement created by Nader would diffuse if they just ignored it.

So when President Lyndon Johnson told the nation in the State of the Union message on January 12 that he planned to "put an end to this mounting tragedy. . .of destruction of life and property on our highways," the sky fell in on Detroit.

In March the White House sent to Congress the Highway Safety Act of 1966, authorizing the Secretary of Commerce to issue safety standards, at his discretion, if after two years the industry hadn't proposed its own. The bill caused a mixed reaction on the hill. To some, like Ribicoff, the bill wasn't strong enough. To others, however, it was at least a step.

"The time has come," Ribicoff told the Senate, "to recognize that safety is not a discretionary matter." He worried that the "imprecise" language of the bill "in the hands of an administration reluctant to be vigorous could offer a basis for no standards at all." The industry, which by that time was lining up lawyers and lobbyists for the coming storm, vehemently contested Ribicoff's opinion that traffic deaths "were a new type of social problem that springs from affluence and abundance rather than from crisis and convulsion."

Nader's case, meantime, was growing stronger. He had allies in Congress and they were eager for more of the same information amassed in *Unsafe*. General Motors realized this, perhaps too well.

On March 9, only seven days after President Johnson had sent his bill to the Congress, the company, in response to several newspaper stories, put out a press release; an unforgettable, regrettable one in the annals of corporate public relations.

In part it read: "General Motors said today that following the publication of Mr. Ralph Nader's criticisms of the Corvair in writings and public appearances in support of his book. . .the Office of the General Counsel instituted a routine investigation. . .limited to Mr. Nader's qualifications, background, expertise and association."

Denying that it had been involved in "harassment or intimidation" of Nader, the $10 billion corporation insisted that it was merely seeking to establish a connection between Nader and a flock of law suits filed against it by *Corvair* owners.

Washington was stunned. So were many people around the country. There were rumors that Nader's sex life was being investigated, his political leanings and even his religion. Was he anti-semitic? If so, Senator Ribicoff might take a different view.

On March 22, Ribicoff reconvened his safety subcommittee and summoned GM president James Roche to explain himself. Before a national TV audience, the stiff, courtly Roche admitted that if he'd known about the surveillance he would have put an end to it before it ever began.

"This investigation was initiated, conducted, and completed without my knowledge or consent and without the knowledge or consent of any of our governing committees. . .to say that I wish I had known about it earlier is an understatement." As the details of the GM surveillance spilled out, under probing from the late Senator Robert F. Kennedy, Roche's explanation seemed, if not misleading, at least seriously incomplete.

As Senator Kennedy bore in on Roche, finally eliciting from him the admission that the investigation wasn't routine, Senator Ribicoff thumbed through the detectives' reports. He

paraphrased some of the findings: "It is apparent. . .that practically none of the investigation had anything to do with what
you contended your investigation was for in your news release of
March 9. Practically no questions were asked of other litigants or
attorneys involved in litigation concerning the Corvair. I know
Winsted, Connecticut. It is a small town in the northwest section
of my state. Detectives invade this small town. . . They go to the
high school principal and start making personal inquiries about a
young man of the town who went to high school. . .and ask
questions whether a man like Ralph Nader was anti-semitic. They
ask questions about his sex habits. . .why isn't a man like this at
his age married. . .before you know it, you have a man who has
led a private and honorable life having reflections cast upon his
entire character, and that of his family, because of these
questions that detectives, who basically aren't sensitive, ask about
a man by the name of Ralph Nader, and this must be happening
all over America with many other Ralph Naders."

As the testimony unfolded, details of General Motors'
strategy toward Nader did, too. After it was announced on
January 17, 1966, that the safety hearings would reopen,
Ribicoff learned that the hometown investigation· mushroomed
into a round-the-clock surveillance in Washington. When Nader
went into a restaurant to eat, detectives saw who he was eating
with and what he ordered for lunch. They got the names of the
taxicabs he was riding in. They followed him when he went into a
bank to make a deposit or a withdrawal. They attempted to
determine what hours he kept. And there were allegations that
girls, in the employ of the detectives, accosted him.

Senator Ribicoff: And would you say that this on behalf of
American business, to say the least, is most unworthy?

Mr. Roche: Yes, I would agree with you, Senator.

Under pressure from Senator Kennedy, Roche blurted:
"This is a new and strange experience for me." Kennedy retorted
a few moments later: "I like my General Motors car, but you
shake me up a little bit."

The hearing was jolted many times that day, as the
tawdry tale was pieced together, a fact at a time. So brazen was
the surveillance that one day the private detectives in GM's
employ followed Nader into the Senate Office Building. That was

their big mistake. An alert reporter heard of the strangers and
flashed the word to his paper.

Nader took his place at the witness chair later in the day.
Kennedy asked him whether he considered the investigation a
harassment. His response:

> I consider it a harassment, Senator, in the context
> that it certainly took up a lot of my time and concern and
> particularly concern over where it was going to end. One can
> possibly take harassing phone calls. One can take surveil-
> lance. But what is quite intolerable is the probings and what
> possibly might be done with these probings. One never
> has a chance to confront the adversary in a sense. It is
> faceless, it is insidious and individuals, not only myself,
> individuals can be destroyed in this manner, quite apart
> from discomfort. And so I was quite fearful of what was
> going to be the end of this. How was this information to be
> used, and whether there was going to be even more overt
> foul play, perhaps of a physical nature.
>
> I am not particularly sensitive to criticism at all. In
> fact I probably have an armor like a turtle when it comes to
> that. I like to give and take. As an attorney one is used to
> it. I don't intimidate easily, but I must confess that one
> begins to have second thoughts of the penalties and the pain
> which must be incurred in working in this area. The thing
> that persuaded me to continue in this area is that I cannot
> accept a climate in this country where one has to have an
> ascetic existence and steely determination in order to speak,
> truthfully, candidly and critically of American industry,
> and the auto industry. I think that if it takes that much
> stamina something is wrong with the enabling climate for
> expression in our country, I don't think that it is generally
> wrong, but I think we need to look into these areas and see
> how we can continually improve this climate. And it goes
> way beyond ideological considerations. This is not an
> ideological problem. This is a problem of individuals con-
> fronting complex organizations, whether they are complex
> organizations in the U.S.—corporations, labor unions or
> what not—or whether they are complex organizations in
> other countries in the world.
>
> The fact is that it is not an equal contest. And as
> long as we recognize, I think the documentation is abun-

dant, that the chief thrust forward in terms of the quality
of our life is almost always associated with individuals
speaking out, I think if we recognize and value that, and I
think we do, because that is one of the touchstones of
our country's claim on history, that we have to go into
it quite meticulously, and see how laws can be improved,
how the public's education can be improved so they can
be aware of these problems, and in effect have a built in
check throughout the society on these types of invasions
of the self and interrogations, and the like.

I think it is not only a matter of law, it is a matter
of awareness of people and their sensitivities to the
rights of individuals, so that when somebody comes in and
probes and just flashes a badge without even showing it,
people don't surrender and say 'I'll tell you everything.'
They will say, 'Who are you? Who do you represent? Who
is your client? Why are you asking these questions? What
is your name? What is your detective serial number?

The impact of the Nader incident is still hotly debated in
Washington. Some legislators, and Nader himself, subscribe to the
view that a safety bill would have passed without the surveillance
episode. Others, however, who are in the majority, believe with
one senior Senator that "all of us were outraged that a great
corporation was out to muzzle a guy because he wrote critically
of them. If there wasn't something wrong with their products,
why did they tail him? At that point, most of us said the hell
with General Motors."

After the incident, the auto companies had no other choice
but to accept some brand of legislation and so by summer, final
bills emerged that were significantly stronger than the formula
proposed by the White House. Rather than allowing the industry
time to establish voluntary standards, the bill signed by President
Johnson on September 9 directed the Commerce Department to
produce mandatory safety standards not only for cars, but for
tires, trucks, and buses and backed it up with civil penalties for
the manufacturers, which Johnson believed were needed to carry
out the spirit of the bill effectively. The industry promised to
"live" with the bill but privately it was no secret that some
companies were making plans to exert influence over the manner
in which the safety standards would be drawn up.

The bill's passage signaled the first breakthrough into the inertia that had surrounded traffic safety since the days of the Model T Ford. Speaker of the House John McCormack offered a public tribute to Nader, crediting the final outcome to the "crusading spirit of one individual who believed he could do something."

By the time the bill was signed, Nader was already widening his horizons and drawing up plans for new assaults against insensitivity about safety and quality in other industries. Auto safety was only a detour from his main crusade: corporate reform.

"In Russia," Nader once told an audience, "the government would be the enemy." But in the U.S. large corporations have emerged as private governments exercising virtually unchecked power over consumers and over the political process. In another speech, titled *Taming the Corporate Tiger*, he declared: "What we do about corporate air and water pollution, corporate soil and food contamination, corporate-bred trauma on our highways, corporate lack of innovation or suppression of innovation, corporate misallocation of resources, inflationary pricing, corporate domination over local, state and Federal agencies—to illustrate a few issues—will decide the quality of our lives."

It was apparent by then that Nader was not just another emotional reformer or muckraker. With a lawyer's mind and the energy of a crusading reporter of the old school, Nader saw a vacuum in Washington that needed filling, that vast area between government and business where battles are often fought not for the goal of improving the quality of life but for ego and money between powerful law firms. There was nothing wrong with these special interests, Nader believed, so long as consumers would be represented in the inner councils as a special interest, too.

As a kind of one-man C.I.A., he learned early that useful information could be sifted from public sources and he spent hours in department libraries gathering data. Out of such forays came fodder for exciting and revealing congressional hearings on the safety of natural gas pipelines crisscrossing the nation and the incidence of x-ray and radiation hazards in diagnostic treatments and TV sets.

As the days went on and as he probed into issue after issue his outrage increased. Various Senators began receiving long detailed memos. "There's a great power to powerlessness," he has said, "I appeal to decency. Sometimes it doesn't work but sometimes it does. If I do it face to face, after a detailed letter to a legislator, it takes a lot of guts for him to look you in the face and say no."

This was the tactic on gas pipelines. A professor of engineering approached him in 1966 and urged him to investigate safety conditions. Horror stories had been circulating in Washington for years about the dangerous condition of gas pipe, much of it implanted many years ago, now corroded and unable to handle modern highpressure flows without exploding.

Nader went underground. He found some dusty government reports and heard of a few people at the Federal Power Commission who were worried about safety. For ten years they'd been fighting to get congressional hearings with no success. Industry pressure on key legislators was too relentless. But Nader began to find a handle, a series of reports in technical journals mentioning explosions, corrosion, and lawsuits. He raced around the country, piecing together an evidentiary case and when he thought he was ready he showed Senate Commerce Committee Chairman Warren Magnuson his work, and made a speech in Washington before the American Society of Safety Engineers. One month later, Magnuson announced hearings. Nader was the first witness. A strong bill emerged from the Senate, giving the states two years to adopt standards and authorizing the Department of Transportation to oversee not only new pipe but the lines that had been there for years. Over in the House the industry, which had been caught offguard in the Senate, gathered forces and softened the bill. But spurred by an unprecedented blast addressed to the House by President Johnson, and constant pressure from Nader and Betty Furness, a compromise bill cleared both houses and was signed by the President in August.

Nader's impact, in part, has been finding new issues, urging legislative exposure and assuring strong administrative watchdogging. But in the meat battle he made a contribution of a different order. Since 1961, Congressmen Neal Smith, Tom Foley and Senator Mondale had frantically tried to secure increased Federal inspection over intrastate packers and processors. For nearly 50 years, 25 per cent of all meat sold, and 15 per cent of all slaughter had gone uninspected. At least eight billion pounds in 1967 escaped Federal inspection, enough for 50 million people. Smith was graphic: "Some of the uninspected plants merely cut the eye out of the cancerous cow, like you would cut the core out of an apple and go ahead and use the rest of the carcass. These uninspected plants, which also process sausages and prepared products can further reduce their costs per pound by including blood, lungs, detergents, hair, hides, antiobotics and excessive amounts of water and flour, without having to label them in such a manner that the consumer would know what he is buying." Despite such an assessment, which at least deserved an examination, Smith could not get the House Agriculture Committee to hold a hearing for six years. But 1967 was a different year. The White House was finding that consumer protection was a potent issue. The costs of the Viet Nam war had created a problem for the President: how to forge a memorable but inexpensive legislative record. In consumer protection he found one. Twelve new bills were sent to Congress, each with warnings attached. In the words of Betty Furness, the chic, unexpectedly effective White House consumer aide who had succeeded Esther Peterson in the job in the spring of 1967, "the consumer is saying 'I no longer want corporations to sit alone in the driver's seat and tell me how it is going to be'."

When he found in the bowels of the Department of Agriculture a little known, state-by-state study of conditions in intrastate meat packing plants, Nader publicized it with the help of Pulitzer Prize winning reporter Nick Kotz, alerted some consumer groups and sparked a letter-writing campaign to the White House and Congress. Then he sat down at his 1915 Remington portable and banged out two hardhitting stories for the *New Republic.* He blamed the entrenchment of outmoded economic ideas for the traffic in what he called "4d—dead, dying, diseased and disabled animals. Ironically, bad meat is, and has been for a long time, good business," he held.

In the fact of the mounting sentiment for strong laws, Aled Davies of the American Meat Institute, the industry's chief lobbyist, tried to be comforting. "We believe generally speaking that (existing) programs have provided the kind of consumer protection in the various states that the people living in these states have thought necessary and have been willing to pay for...We wonder whether the benefits to be gained (from a law that would require state plants to be inspected) justify the kind of Federal expenditures that could develop."

L. Blaine Liljenquist of the Western States Meat Packers, for his part, was entirely against any legislation. The National Association of State Departments of Agriculture took a similar stance by offering amendments to the House bill that would have eviscerated it.

Nader wasn't getting much help from the U.S. Department of Agriculture, either. In July, 1967, after digging out the long-hidden surveys, Nader sought out several department officials and asked them if there were any other reports. They told him that there were not. By then, Nader was on to them anyway, in particular as a result of laboratory tests of meat products from intrastate plants made in 1967. Of 162 samples, 123 didn't meet Federal standards. Such giant, non-fly-by-nighters as Armour and Swift were found to be sprinkling beef with powdered charcoal for sausages.

A legislative scuffle before a strong bill was passed found the White House and Agriculture Secretary Freeman in disagreement at times over whether the bill should allow the states to handle the regulation or permit the government to give the states a warning, some extra time, and only then move to assure that no shortcuts were being taken. But Nader, along with Betty Furness and Senator Mondale, prodded the White House into backing a stronger bill. He had some help, too. The mail pouring into the White House was overwhelmingly in favor of the strongest possible bill. Some of the mail was from meat inspectors and their wives. Betty Furness, for her part, was appalled to discover that some of the largest food chains—Safeway, A&P, Kroger, First National—sold meat adulterated with water, chemicals, and cereals.

If the consumer protectionists had written the screenplay, they couldn't have cast themselves in a nobler role. The meat industry got the kind of bill it wanted from the House, what Nader called a "no-law law," only to be ambushed at the Senate pass by Nader and his consumer legion. Wrote Stanley Cohen, chief of *Advertising Age*'s Washington Bureau: "The consumer forces, with a few murderous strokes, turned the battle into

another disaster for the food industry, still struggling to recover consumer good will lost in the fight over 'Truth in Packaging'."

By the time the Senate and House had worked out a bill for the President's signature, on December 15, 1967, the meat industry had won for itself the villain's role, as millions of Americans saw their providers fight for the right to sell rotten meat to them. The issue cut through to the kitchens of consumers across the nation, for what was involved was not only dishonest labeling, but safety and health.

Sensing the climate, President Johnson staged an elaborate signing ceremony in the East Room of the White House. In attendance was Upton Sinclair, a host of highranking government officials and dozens of Congressmen, many of them the ones who had opposed the bill until the end but now wanted to bathe in the reflected glory of another victory for the American consumer. Election time was coming.

The President made the most of the moment. First he quoted a passage from *The Jungle* of 1906, written by Sinclair, describing rotten meat.

"Then listen to this," he said. " 'A man was wrapping pork shoulders. He dropped one in the sawdust, picked it up and wiped it off with a dirty, sour rag. . .Beef was being broken on an open dock, by a dirt road, in 95-degree weather. There were flies on the meat. Drums of bones and meat scraps were covered with maggots.' What I just read you was not from *The Jungle*. It did not happen 60 years ago when Upton Sinclair was writing his book. It happened in July 1967. It was written by a United States Government inspector after a visit to one of our great, modern packing plants. We are here this morning to make sure that that plant will either clean up or close down. We have waited a long time for this bill.

"Upton Sinclair's book spurred the public to fight for a clean meat bill. They got a clean meat bill—the Meat Inspection act of 1907.

"President Theodore Roosevelt said it would 'insure wholesomeness from the hoof to the can'.

"But that bill did only a very small part of the job. It covered only meat that crossed state lines.

"That left a gap. It did not protect our families against 8-3/4 billion pounds of meat that receive no Federal inspection.

That is enough meat to feed 50 million people. That is 15 per cent of all the fresh meat that is sold—and that is 25 per cent of all the processed meat products sold—in this entire country. This doesn't mean that all, or even half, of that meat in any way is tainted—or suspect. But—it does mean that somewhere there are some packers who have been peddling meat from '4D' animals—dead, dying, disabled and diseased.

—it does mean that these shady processors—whoever and wherever they may be—have been allowed to operate some filthy plants in this country and one filthy plant is one too many.

—it does mean we are risking the health of our children and our families. This is an intolerable condition in the 20th century in a modern nation that prides itself on reputed leadership of the world."

Once again Nader had helped put the spotlight on the gap between what was possible, indeed, what most people thought was the condition and what was the actual. Slowly, Nader was writing new guidelines for corporate behavior and slowly, millions of consumers discovered that maybe he wasn't a crackpot after all but a man who had chosen a life in which his own problems, everyday difficulties of survival, had been subjugated to the problems of society. Even some of his legislative enemies have come to admire him—at a distance. Lloyd Cutler, a Washington lawyer and lobbyist who represented the auto industry told an interviewer early in 1968:

"He's an important and effective social and political force but he'd be more effective if he were charitable of the motives and integrity of the people he attacks." Nader's rejoinder: "Considering the problems I think I am very charitable."

Nader's allies at least are convinced that he's for real, that what motivates him is not deep hatred of businessmen or of the free enterprise system. That's the poignancy of it. Nader's a deep believer in the system. Yet he wants it to work better. "Men like Ralph who have a very strong sense of professional responsibility are something this country lacks," says urbanist Daniel Moynihan.

Beyond his impact on specific legislation, Nader has exerted another kind of influence on Capitol Hill. As a powerful Senate Counsel explained it to an interviewer, "Ralph has pricked the conscience of many Congressional staff members. He has had almost a religious influence on us, and I use the word carefully, I hate to call myself a convert, but today I am more inclined to look at whether or not a piece of legislation serves the public interest. In large part, this is because Ralph has time after time raised the moral issues involved in the bills that come before us. "It's easy for Congressmen and their staffs to succumb to the Washington milieu. The industry lobbyists are chosen because they are charming and persuasive men. The Senator or Representative knows that consumer protection isn't good politics; the private interests are organized and the public isn't. It's easy to go along. What Ralph has done is force a lot of people to face facts, and to remember that they're here to represent the people."

If Nader has a major fault it is that he sizes people up too quickly, along ideological lines and won't allow them time to mellow and come around to his view. His opponents chip away at him on the grounds that he's hoisting himself on his own petard. One lobbyist explains: "Nader worries me. He's got the best of both worlds. He asks 'who decides' and then he does. Isn't that just what he says insensitive board chairmen do? He's not responsible to anyone and that concerns me. The public is being defended all right without Ralph."

Just as many others are concerned about Nader, too, but not for the same reasons. "I hope nothing happens to him," a Johnson administration official told a friend. There is, in fact, justification for that brand of concern. Nader may be trying to tackle too many issues at once, from oil depletion allowances to mine safety, conglomerate mergers to sonic boom and if he is to survive, he needs help. But such an idea poses a problem. Before Nader will employ anyone in the public interest law firm he has on the drawing boards, not only must he have complete confidence in him but also be assured that 100-hour weeks will be tolerable. Nader works the hours of a jewel thief on the Riviera. If he is to continue, however, Nader must take a chance on employees. The pilot program now on the drawing boards is budgeted at $250,000 a year. With that amount he could rent a larger office, hire two or three secretaries, and maintain a permanent staff of lawyers, accountants, engineers, economists, and doctors. The firm would provide a third voice in the legislative fracas on Capitol Hill, the "real voice" in congressional hearings and at regulatory meetings.

As Fred Zimmerman wrote in the *Wall Street Journal*, "the thought of a well-financed Ralph Nader surely may give pause to some government officials and industry lobbyists, in view of what he has been able to accomplish with limited funds."

These accomplishments, helping to establish priorities for health and safety issues, present a serious dilemma because Nader has created armies of enemies who are watching from a distance like wolves on the edge of the wood, waiting for him to stumble and fall.

Many of his followers thought that happened during a Congressional hearing in the summer of 1968 when he charged that some dentists had been overexposing patients to x-rays with machines that were sometimes unsafe. Negroes, he said, occasionally received larger doses because dentists and doctors thought their heads were thicker than the skulls of white people. True? It sounded like a wild charge. The American Dental Association dashed for cover and assembled a barrage of denials. Then, a few days later, a top official of the Department of Health, Education and Welfare surfaced with a confirmation of Nader's basic charge. Reporters were supplied with substantiating evidence.

As Nader prowls on for further examples of imbalances in the American industrial society of the 1960s, he is far less lonely than when he first arrived in 1964. A systematic effort has begun to put President John Kennedy's four consumer rights of 1962 into practice. In the strictest sense, there's been no revolution but a consumer protection movement has been evolving, led by Nader, Furness and a few others and the movement has far from lost its steam. At least Nader doesn't think so. "I haven't really begun my work yet," he said a few months ago. Few would believe him but Nader insists that he wishes his presence were not needed. "If businessmen were evil," he once explained, "there would be no need for anyone like me. The laws take care of obvious crooks. But businessmen are not evil. They are sometimes insensitive and are victimized by the large corporations which employ them. Soon they become insensitive to the world about them. There are no laws to deal with insensitive people. The problem, for example, is not whether the oil and auto industries can build a smog-free car, it's whether the opposition of those two industries can be overcome to get it built."

The Sane Sell

chapter 6

"...I'll tell you the secret of the soap business, Mr. Norman. There's no damn difference between soap. Except for perfume and color, soap is soap. Oh maybe we get a few manufacturing tricks but the public don't give a damn about that. The difference is the selling and the advertising...we sell soap twice as fast as our nearest competitor because we outadvertise them."

The Hucksters, 1946

"Advertising has been denied for privilege of the big lie...but it still makes use of flat statements that are never proved, assertions that turn out upon careful examination not to be declarations at all but only carefully structured inferences and spirited and striking comparisons."

Emerson Foote, Industry pioneer, 1967

"...they go into a little confessional-size booth and look into a box where they see either slides or commercials and while they are looking a sensitive camera is taking pictures of their left eyeballs every half second...Marplan pupillometrics expert Paul Drillman supplied the information that the average consumer's pupil is two millimeters in diameter— small pupils bad reaction, big pupils good reactions."

The New York Times, 1968

If there were a contest for the socio-economic whipping boy championship of the post-war decades, the $17 billion advertising industry would win it in a landslide. No sector of the nation's at once magnificent and perplexing marketplace has borne more whipsaw criticism or towering tirade. With random abandon sociologists, novelists and economists have hacked and trampled through the vineyards where the shrill commercials are stored.

Inevitably, Hollywood grasped the scenario in the 1950s and 1960s, transforming the earlier novels into forgettable films. Everyone had a field day except industry leaders who scampered from thicket to thicket, ducking the rhetorical fusillades, to no avail. Against J. K. Galbraith's critique that advertising was "wasteful" and the taunts of Arnold Toynbee that it was "evil," counterattack was ineffective. As the industry hurtled into the mid-sixties, the ancient hucksters' art was being blamed for everything from the four-hour lunch to the general decline of American morals, and most industry caliphs had acquired a highly-developed persecution complex. For the beleaguered buyer this was a calamitous development; the battle with the seller would rage on with no truce in sight.

But as the nation approaches the 1970s a truly different assault is being launched by the forces of the third consumer movement of the 20th century, a more meaningful exchange which is neither the stuff of fiction nor grist for Hollywood tinsel factories. The result may be the implementation of a concept which smacked, heretofore, of bolshevism to admen: advertising, if it is to survive, must become the authentic voice of the consumer even though it is paid for by the producer. This is no evangelical postulation by Ralph Nader or White House consumer adviser Betty Furness. The author is Paul Foley, Chairman of McCann-Erickson, the world's second largest agency with 1967 billings of $476 million.

After a series of stormy legislative skirmishes in Washington, the anciently lopsided balance of power is slowly shifting from the seller to the buyer. Mr. Foley and a covey of his peers have heard the beat of the new drum and intend to head off further embarassment in the spotlight of exposure and black headlines. The new cadence: controlling the consumer with psychological legerdemain, cannonading him with barrages of vulgarity, idiocy, condescension and deception by omission is not merely undesirable in a world of unmanaged, monumental abundance. It is no longer tolerable in a society which has decided to erradicate pollution and poverty.

The American consumer must realize when he reads of Ralph Nader's exploits that something most certainly is wrong with a system that allows unsafe drugs and cars and rotten meat to be sold. And he may also realize that what men like writer Dexter Masters have been writing for years is alarmingly more germane to his predicament than the blithe abstractions delivered by the academic sharpshooters in Galbraith's legions.

"The intelligent buyer," Masters has written, "must be alert to every commercial sound, to every snapping of a selling twig, to every rustle that may signal the uprising arm holding the knife pointed toward the jugular vein."

It was during Shakespeare's lifetime that advertising as the most visible arm of the seller took shape. "Let me have no lying," the Bard once carped, "It becomes none but tradesmen."* By the middle of the eighteenth century, the arm was rising. In 1758, Dr. Samuel Johnson noted in the *Idler* that "advertisements are now so numerous that they are very negligently perused and it has therefore become necessary to gain attention by the magnificence of promises and by eloquence sometimes sublime and sometimes pathetic. Promise—large promise—is the soul of advertising."

As the commercial revolution unfolded, watching the arm rising higher was Charles Dickens. His cynical watchwords to the buyer: "Here's the rule for bargains: do other men, for they would do you, that's the true business concept." If only these able penmen could observe the current marketplace, transistorized, electrified to the hilt, awash with large economy sizes, possessing secret, distinctive special ingredients and then unsheath again their pens. Oh *Joy*! Oh *Ice Blue Secret*!

There are indications that advertising is coming down to earth after decades of aloofness punctuated with belligerency toward both the consumer and voices of reform. It is doubtful whether the current president of the American Association of Advertising would tell an annual meeting, as one of his

*From the play "The Winter's Pale," Act 4, Scene 3, Line 747.

... William Shakespeare

predecessors did some years ago that everyone should "stop worrying about every piddling criticism of our business. If there is any collective quality of the public, it's indifference." And in today's climate, market researcher Alfred Politz would have to temper the assessment he once made of the industry's role: "The solution to marketing problems is not one of giving consumers what they want, but rather to make consumers want what we, the marketers, want them to want."

An operative national goal for advertising was framed by President John Kennedy in 1962. Protection for consumers must include self-protection and they cannot achieve self-protection unless they know the facts and use them. That prefaced his famous consumer message, which stated in part that "if consumers are offered inferior products, if prices are exorbitant, if drugs are unsafe or worthless. If the consumer is unable to choose on an informed basis, then his dollar is wasted, his health and safety may be threatened and the national interest suffers."

When it has the potential to penetrate the marketplace with relevant information the consumerists are appalled at the industry's apparent determination to promote and nurture a system which rewards those who can confuse the consumer the most. A spokesman for the school of mindboggling repetition, an executive for Fuller, Smith and Ross counseled a gathering of admen a few years ago. "If you engage in anything short of a direct assault on the jugular vein, you are in the Mickey Mouse league."

Long before the arrival of television, the medium that has revolutionized the assault, industry pioneer Raymond Rubicam posed an even more basic tenet: "The object of advertising is to sell. It has no other justification."

In all deference to Mr. Rubicam who, with Mr. Young, founded a dazzlingly successful agency, such an analysis today would send him not only into the bush leagues but put him in deep left field. Shouts and hoots would come not just from consumerists but even from advertising leaders themselves. The new theme: the old ways may have been successful but they are not necessarily the best ways. In May 1968 American Advertising Federation president Howard Bell explained to a convention of his peers: "Advertising is a vital industry that needs some revitalizing. It's in the business of persuading and it has considerable persuading to do in its own cause."

It is next to impossible to fix the precise time when advertising ceased to be a means of spreading real detail about products and became a force of persuasion, but now that consumer alienation is growing some serious thinking is being done within the industry to achieve a more balanced approach. "We must hold ourselves responsible for truthfulness and good taste," says J. Walter Thompson Chairman Norman Strouse, "If we cannot police ourselves in these areas, we are simply tempting the legislative fates that are often more severe than the ailment they attempt to cure."

What is now required in this era of consumerism, is that advertising be evaluated not only as a selling tool but whether it serves its function in a broader social context. At a time in history of unparalleled consumer prosperity the consumer is growing restless and confused because the simple act of purchase has become an increasingly impersonal experience. The contest between buyer and seller is unequal in many sectors of the economic system but rarely more so than in advertising. Acknowledging this, consumer spokesmen such as Betty Furness and Ralph Nader suggest a start toward evaluating advertising in terms of its effect on the consumer as well as on the profits of the producer.

The consumer's problem around the world, especially in the U.S., is that relevant information is scarce. The consumerists protest that white tornadoes whipping across kitchen floors or giants billowing up from washing machines simply don't give the buyer a fighting chance.

"The marketplace is pushing too many products for the typical consumer to make sensible value judgments," declares Betty Furness. "Few housewives are able to carry slide rules with them to the supermarket but that's what they need to determine the best buy in products like toothpaste that offer 57 different sizes in a 16 ounce range."

Can the consumer be protected from a daily bombardment of tiresome repetitions, overstatements and competitive absurdities? Should he be? Now that most of the nation's institutions are being brought under the analytical spotlight and as the society becomes increasingly interdependent, the answer the consumerists put forth is a loud affirmative. Controlling the consumer or at least inhibiting his choice is no longer accepted as an inevitable consequence of an affluent society, especially now that numerous government reports indicate that the relative absence of buying information compounds the problem of poverty in the nation's ghettoes.

The consumerists have initiated a broad re-examination which recognizes that advertising by itself is merely an instrument and a concomitant effect of broader ills lurking in the system. Since the first copywriter poised his stylus over a blank papyrus in ancient Thebes 3000 years ago advertising's essential *raison d'etre* has been to encourage, indeed fight for, the favorable acceptance of a product, an idea, or an institution. This process has not always been synonymous with candor on the part of the seller. The advertiser has always claimed that the consumer has received abundant information. Such industry proponents as publisher Herbert Mayes have further added that consumers don't utilize the information they do get. "They don't read more," he once noted, "because they happen to believe in the quality and the value of most of the products they buy and in the integrity of the companies whose trademarks are on them." Mayes' real point: if consumers are entitled to more information then industry is best suited to provide it, on its own terms.

Just what consumer information should be is the target of the battle now being waged. When Betty Furness suggests that a buyer should be told how long his new icebox will last, advertising men skitter off into small groups and talk of the "bombthrowers" in Washington. It's safe to say Miss Furness is no longer "sure-if-it's-Westinghouse."

The report to the White House by the Consumer Advisory Council in 1966 set the rules of battle for the re-evaluation. In middle-class, twentieth century America, almost every shopper confronts an impressive selection of new products and new versions of old products. Getting information is almost as difficult for the well-to-do consumer as for the poorly educated and the poor. "The consumer today," the report lamented, "must be chemist, electrician and nutritionist to fathom what he is buying, what it will do, how well it will perform and endure and how to take care of it."

What the outriders of consumerism are demanding in short is not that advertising relinquish its cherished freedom to sell the way it wants to sell. They are offering a choice: either make a determined effort to aid the consumer in his agony of wonder and perplexity or batten down the hatches for new laws which nobody wants. Regulation and responsibility, in short, are the price of freedom.

In one sense the battle between the buyer and the seller is not much different from what it always has been—uneven, one-sided, confusing for the buyer and profitable for the seller. Yet as the society grows more complex the information gap grows wider and the repair problem becomes a nightmare of wasted telephone calls and dishonored warranties. Questions about relative tire performance, brake stopping distances, the performance and durability of hundreds of modern gadgets, from color TV sets to 20-speed blenders frequently go unanswered in an avalanche of sexy, vacuous commercials. The dreary technique of emotional appeal still holds center stage.

What the advertising industry may just now be sensing is that its high-decibel diet is colliding with the consumer's growing sense of rising expectations. He wants more than a commercial for an American Motors car showing the salesman impaled by a javelin. His desire, as indicated by a flood of letters to the White House, Congress, and Ralph Nader is to be treated as a mature, rational individual with a genuine need, born of past disappointment, to participate intelligently in the marketplace. That need embraces the ability to make purposeful decisions about the myriad choices that the marketplace offers and to act on the basis of knowledge and self-interest.

The meteoric rate of changing technology, the endless innovations that have tumbled forth from laboratories, factories and ad agencies have paradoxically played a role in creating the industry's current crisis of confidence. The faster technology changes and the more products generated the more outmoded oldfashioned sales and marketing practices become. During the metamorphosis, the task of buying intelligently has grown ever more perplexing, due to the changing character of the products as much as to the shrill advertisements that sell them. No longer does the marketplace provide staples of known material—flour, woolens, axe handles—which a consumer can buy based on his experience and his knowledge of its value and longevity. Nowadays, the majority of products are made of so many synthetic materials than even a trained technician must struggle to decide the relative merits of an array of similar products. The efforts of Consumers Union to arm the buyer undoubtedly have averted much grief and handwringing but in the view of Washington consumer vigilantes, those efforts have had limited impact.

The root of the problem, Federal Trade Commission Chairman Paul Rand Dixon believes, is that "consumers are often unable to bring personal knowledge to bear in making purchases and usually must rely on what a remote manufacturer in an advertisement says his product will do." The Commission, with a minute budget, is hardly able to effectively slow the tide of inferior products hurtling into the marketplace enhanced by whitty jingles and clever omissions.

John Kenneth Galbraith, for one, doesn't believe that the industry will reform. Instead he sees its main drive as a rush toward control of the consumer by not providing the sort of pertinent information that would equalize the bargaining positions. University of California philosophy professor Henrick Skolinowski puts it more strongly. "For many admen 'freedom' means freedom to advertise in whatsoever manner is profitable, freedom to force you to buy, freedom to penetrate your subconscious, freedom to dupe you, to hook you, to make a sucker of you, freedom to take away your freedom."

A series of questionable ad compaigns in 1967 illustrate some of the modern pitfalls of sophisticated ads, consumers should be aware of. Each tested the Federal Trade Commission's authority and inclination to "prohibit unfair methods of competition in commerce and unfair and deceptive acts or practices in commerce."

In a national Shell Oil ad, two cars cruised along East Side Drive in Manhattan. One car was powered with the much ballyhooed platformate, the other by just plain gas. Soon the car without platformate sputtered, grunted once or twice and stopped, while the other purred onward to its destination. A misleading ad? Shell argued that it wasn't. Even though any oil and gas industry man knows that all gas contains platformate, the real message Shell said, was that the car with Shell gas from which platformate had been removed didn't run as well as the car fueled by platformate-added gas. Confusing? Not at all except that most gas companies exchange gas with each other to prevent supply and demand problems and there's little difference between any of the brands. While Shell's product may not have been better or different from its competitors, consumers were quite taken with the campaign, to the extent that during the eight years since Shell started tubthumping special ingredients, its share of the U.S. market has jumped 6 per cent to 8.4 per cent of the total.

To government officials who noticed the Shell ad but didn't take action for budgetary and perhaps political reasons, the claims of the platformate campaign reminded them of the baker who claimed a secret ingredient for his bread: Flour.

In the drug advertising field, misleading campaigns are far more damaging to the confused buyer than the Shell ad. A sample of ads sifted from the Federal Drug Administration's investigative docket reveals that the consumerists are not shooting blanks.

Item: A heavily advertised drug, the ad campaign for which claimed that no serious kidney or nervous disorders resulted but which failed to report that a unique feature of the dosage was "frequency of severe diarrhea."

Item: An ad for an angina pectoris preparation, relying on a study to imply a claim of efficacy without specifying that the study had not been done on humans but on piglets.

Item: A paid entry in a drug-prescribing guide that failed to include this information—the anti-diabetic product had in large doses killed and deformed animal fetuses.

One of the oldest gambits advertising agencies try to employ is an ad placed in a publication in the guise of news. It's hardly a new phenomenon; the *London Tatler*, in 1714, chastised local London tradesmen for the practice.

Only recently, Colgate-Palmolive, one of the nation's largest companies got some mileage from what has been called the "advertorial" during the introduction of a new hardwater soap called *Punch*. Side by side in hundreds of newspapers around the country there appeared ads for *Punch* and a news story which cited an authoritative report that hard water existed in the area. A consumer's windfall? Not exactly, because the ad and the news story both had been prepared by the same copywriter. By one estimate, advertorials accounted for 10 percent of the budget Colgate-Palmolive allotted for the introduction of *Punch*.

In a similar case, the old and trusted *Reader's Digest* carried a special section in its November 1967 issue, advocating brand-name drugs over the lower priced, generic versions of the same preparations. Except for some fine print on the last page of the fat section, there was no way the reader could tell that the "story" was written by the Pharmaceutical Manufacturers Association. Of course, it wasn't an objective news story at all. The U.S. Post Office promptly accused the *Digest* of violating second-class mailing rules. The *Digest* quickly apologized. Many months later, the P.M.A. did, too.

Deceptive advertising has always been part of the industry's fabric, no less so today than in other days. In the past when, as FTC Chairman Paul Rand Dixon has put it, "the foxes were caught sneaking into the chicken coop," the typical defense was either that the rigors of competition or the inexact rules of the game—or both—were the true villains. Such a position now still gets a hearing but more frequently such rhetoric is falling on deaf ears in Washington. Instead, several powerful voices at the FTC have suggested that if the industry can't police itself perhaps the answer lies in affixing full warranty status to all advertising copy.

Others, such as Phil Elman, considered by many the most brilliant FTC commissioner in years, take a different tack. Spotting the split personality of the industry, Elman doesn't quarrel with the idea that advertising has been but a sales tool and not a fountain of relevant information. But, he says, "when advertising does purport to convey information the least that can be expected is that the information given be accurate. We should all be concerned by the tendency of some advertisers to walk as close to the line separating legal from illegal advertising claims. The result is a barrage of puffery and misinformation that undermines the credibility of all advertisers in the eyes of the public and lends support to those who propose government action requiring advertising to be more informative."

"How often," he asks, "do we see advertisements extolling the 'secret,' 'distinctive' or 'special' ingredient of a product when in fact it is chemically identical to competing products and the so-called 'secret ingredient' is present in all of them, perhaps under different names?"

To be sure, many advertising men will admit without much prodding that their standards could and should be higher. But what angers the consumerists is that these same men assign most of the problems to the fringe areas. The way the industry's critics see it, the industry's problems exist right at the core. A majority of large companies have been cited by the F.T.C. for crossing the line.

While the debate continues about the degree of deception, the FTC is being inundated with complaints of false and misleading ads. Each year thousands pour in. They range from deceptive automobile blurbs to toothpaste commercials, aspirin to fur coats.

Operating under the broadest charter of any present agency, the FTC emerges as the reluctant policeman of the industry; with a tiny annual budget, one fourth the annual ad spending of Procter and Gamble, it hardly has tiger's teeth. But chairman Dixon is determined to snap, nonetheless.

Reflecting on the agency's role recently, Dixon stated that "it takes no great clairvoyance to predict why false advertising cases will continue to flood the commission. It will be because too many advertisers, with or without the connivance of their agencies, and without or against the advice of their lawyers, will take a change on trading truth for more sales. These firms are going to gamble that bigger profits will outweigh the combined dangers of dissatisfied customers and vengeful competitors and state and local authorities. And the sad fact is that some of them will succeed." With a touch of venom in his voice, Dixon thundered, in deep Southern tones, "The day of *caveat venditor* is here—let the seller beware and that includes advertisers."

Even if much of today's advertising is misleading, what damage does it do to the consumer? It could be argued that most TV viewers, for example, simply wink at the outrageously infantile fare they are fed during prime time. Stan Freberg, the sometime satirist and magnificently successful copywriter, insists that people go to the bathroom during commercials. As proof he cites a suppressed research report an agency once prepared which revealed that the water level in a certain mid-west town dropped sharply at 15 and 30 minutes past the hour during prime time. No Madison Avenue pawns were they.

More than twenty years ago, Bruce Barton, an industry pioneer, excused its shortcomings as inconsequential:

"We are not so blind as to be unaware of our faults. We confess frankly that advertising is young, that it has grown so fast that its greatest need is better trained executives; and that it has grave shortcomings. But so has every finite institution. If advertising persuades some men to live beyond their means, so does matrimony. If advertising speaks to a thousand in order to influence one, so does the church. If advertising is so often garrulous and redundant and tiresome, so is the U.S. Senate.

"We are young and law and medicine and theology are old. Yet in our business practice, by and large, I venture to assert that we need not be ashamed to be measured beside even these great professions, and we claim for ourselves, as they claim for themselves, the right to be measured not by our worst but by our best."

But as the industry approaches the 1970's, youth is no longer an excuse. It is running headlong into the effects of the juxtaposition of an old Chinese proverb, that now the seller not the buyer, needs a thousand eyes, and the buyer but one.

The advocates of consumerism are not about to suggest that advertising should be restricted from etching pictures of far-off Shangri-las where bulldogs all have rubber teeth. But what they are asking is that more attention be paid to truth and reason.

A first step, Paul Rand Dixon believes is for the industry to remove the large chip that has rested on its shoulder for years. "Advertising suffers from one of its own maxims—its image must always be a positive one—never negative. Never cast a shadow of a doubt that advertising ever falls short of serving an exalted purpose—bringing the rich life to all and powering the wheels of industry." The problem, however, is that "some advertising serves the opposite purpose. It is the water in the milk. Yet, rather than invite government assistance in halting those who would dilute their product, they cling to the idea that advertising's image would suffer." Dixon's advice: "Quit worrying about what government agencies might do to advertising's image and worry more about whether performance entitles it to a good image."

As the industry with all its dynamism and creativity careens into the most challenging period it has ever faced, there remains a very real question whether reform is possible, given the state of hostility between itself and government. Advertising Federation President Bell agrees: "We need a new approach which will lead to a further de-escalation in hostilities. Government should cease provoking business by engaging in wholesale name-calling in its zeal to indict a few. Business should stop overreacting by treating every government action as the Battle of the Bulge. . . with this kind of clearing of the air, the real mutuality of our interest should become more apparent and an era of cooperation can replace one of hostility and suspicion. We may at times decry the false labels of the consumerism movement and the political exploitation of this attractive and appealing banner but we cannot deny its existence. We must accept the fact that there are problems and they are not going to be wished away."

What the consumerists have been conveying to the advertising industry is that no destructive attack is looming or is even desired. No useful purpose would be served. The thrust of the consumerists' platform: seek a middle ground of accommodation. The government is saddled with too much detail and budget deficiences so the onus is on the industry to heal itself. Unfortunately, however, the dominant reaction is constructed of the stuff of *laissez-faire* dogma; government is the real enemy of freedom of information in the marketplace and poses a threat that will eventually result in economic hardships for producers and higher prices for the consumer.

There is no question that ad men have a point when they stress need for brand name reliability in this period of unprecedented consumer mobility, even if higher prices result. Most consumerists only wish that more attention was paid to forewarning these mobile consumers about new products in different regions of America. Advertising, in short, performs little or no service in this respect.

It is not difficult to understand why the industry is currently enmeshed in an identity crisis, for it has come a great distance in a few short years in terms of its impact on the nation. Until 40 years ago, in fact, advertising was a minor force. Total spending in 1900, for example, was less than $200 million. A few years later Albert Lasker and his fellow pioneers began to define advertising as "salesmanship in print" and the "reason why" school of advertising was born. It's aim was to convince the consumer that the product was infinitely in his or her interest.

One needs to recall that advertising, in today's form is new, but as a selling tool is a thousand years old. Perhaps that's the key to the rising level of intolerance among the nation's consumers.

Archeologists have unearthed the remains of outdoor signs in the ruins of ancient civilizations. The first ads appeared in the U.S. in 1704 in the Boston News-Letter. A plantation and two anvils were put up for sale. But it was not until the 1880's that advertising emerged in the U.S. as a distinct industry. The pump was primed by the growth of the department store, the birth of the commercial detergent business and the patent medicine industry. Even in these days, unsophisticated as they were, there was concern about the misleading quality of some ads.

In 1880 the editors of the Farm Journal wrote:

"We believe, through careful inquiry, that all advertisements in this paper are signed by trustworthy persons and to prove our faith by works we will make good to subscribers any less sustained by trusting advertisers who prove to be deliberate swindlers. Rogues shall not ply their trade at the expense of our readers who are our friends."

The plight of the industry remains unchanged. Abuses exist but who shall curb them? Since 1912 the industry has attempted to police itself, with varying degrees of success, through a network of Better Business Bureaus. The very first case of deceptive claims was revealing in the sense that the issues haven't changed much.

Following the Pure Food and Drug hearings of 1906, which revealed deep abuses in the marketing system, the government filed a rash of law suits against a number of companies, including *Coca Cola*. During the trial company sales manager Sam Dobbs sat quietly by as a U.S. attorney charged *Coca Cola* with false and misleading advertising. "That was annoying enough," Dobbs recalled later, "but what shocked me was the way our attorney responded to the charge."

"Why, all advertising is exaggerated, nobody really believes it," the attorney protested with a wave of his hand.

Dobbs was stunned. He soon discovered that other advertising men were worried, too. Events unfolded rapidly. Dobbs was elected president of the Advertising Clubs of America in 1909 (now the Advertising Federation of America). The post provided him with a mandate to begin a campaign of self-regulation. Two years later ten commandments for truth in advertising were unveiled. Later the same year Printers Ink publisher John Romer organized a group of vigilance committees designed to function at the local and regional levels. The network evolved in the National Better Business bureaus of today.

Unfortunately, like much of advertising itself, the Better Business Bureau approach is outmoded and anachronistic. Advertising has shifted to national campaigns away from local and regional marketing but the BBB still chases the billboard deceptions and as such has little impact on the root of the problem. When a major tire company in a national compaign deliberately portrays its tires as strong four-ply models, when in fact two-ply is what the new car buyer gets, the BBB's hardly make a peep,

When the BBB's began to organize, Princeton professor Walter Scott Dill, spotting the inconsistency wrote that "there is no force in America that can suppress fraudulent advertising and thus win the confidence of the public. . .except the advertisers themselves." That is ever true today.

With the advent of radio in the 1920s the rising arm was electrified and thus became more deadly, what with the hard-sell repetitive pitches of George Washington Hill for *Lucky Strike* and Henry Ford's *Model-T*. The progression from those early, successful beginnings to today's diet is a straight line. The automobile, with the attendant implications of freedom, offered mobility and advertising fanned the flames with men of distinction, travel to far off places, the girls who dream they are queens if they wear a maidenform bra, magic cleansers and cars that fly through the air.

That however is not the world of today, as Corn Products chairman A.N. McFarlane said recently.

"Beyond question, the emerging ethics are challenging business orthodoxy. What concerns me is how the business community may respond to these ethical changes. It would be a grave error to view them as only a threat, something to resist. As I see it, they are an expression of public thinking which we attack or disregard only at great peril. . .we have to decide whether, in the marketplace for ideas, we will allow ourselves to become alienated from the mainstream of public thought."

"We can respond," McFarlane went on, "to the new emphasis on the quality of life—as opposed to the quantity of things—not only by modifying our product mix, but by more sensitive handling of business actions and communications—advertising included."

An even more emphatic plea for enlightened response has come from International Business Machines board chairman Thomas Watson: "If we businessmen insist that free enterprise permits us to be indifferent to those things on which people put high value, then the people will quite naturally assume that free enterprise has too much freedom." Clearly while quite a few company chieftains may be seeing and charting the future the word has yet to pass to the marketing departments. All too few advertising campaigns are able to reconcile the realties of mid-20th century social and industrial upheaval with the ancient hard sell.

With keen prescience, consumer crusader Ralph Nader summed up advertising's modern challenge: the need to be revelant. At a crucial point in the traffic safety hearings in March, 1966, Senator Robert Kennedy asked Nader why he was fighting so hard for safety. Nader replied that he had looked at many auto industry advertisements in his research, "which boasted," he said, "of how advanced and sophisticated and progressive their scientific engineering research and applications are and perhaps it is because I tried to believe some of that, I was shocked when I saw the drastic gap between the performance of the industry and its promise."

Reconciling appearance with reality, then, is one of the tasks ahead for advertising, as it is for much of the U.S. industrial establishment. No doubt dramatic improvements in ethics and self-regulation have taken place since the days the food packagers sold half-poisoned peas as the personification of the new leisure. The trouble with self-regulation is that much of it has been aimed, critics say, more at protecting industry from crooks and malfeasers than insulating the consumer against deception.

The problem of deception, in the opinion of Harvard professor Donald Turner, former head of the Justice Department's anti-trust division, runs secondary to advertising's basic fault. "It has failed to provide consumers," he once said, "with anywhere near the kind and amount of information they need in order to make intelligent choices among competing products." Moreover, the industry's practices materially interfere with effective competition in consumer goods markets. "While advertising comprises an important form of rivalry among firms, this form is likely to be considerably different in economic effect from those forms of economic competition which are concerned with prices established in the market. Heavy advertising outlays lead both to more concentrated market structures and to the establishment of high-monopolistic prices."

Strong fare. Turner's evidence: the four largest soap companies, also the four heaviest advertisers, control 74 per cent of the marketplace even though government studies have shown, all soap contains essentially the same ingredients.

The chance for the Turner case ever being tried is far less than the advertising industry believes; other matters such as what to do about cigarette advertising are now taking precedent. And if the advertising and tobacco's industry reaction to the 1964 Surgeon General's report, connecting smoking with cancer and heart disease, is any sample of how it intends to respond to consumerism, the future of Washington-advertising relations is dark, indeed.

Even after the 1964 report, it took a convulsive struggle in Congress to produce the mild warning now required on every cigarette pack: "Caution: cigarette smoking may be hazardous to your health." The Federal Trade Commission, after waiting until June, 1968 to detect signs of responsiveness to the health problem from tobacco companies and their ad agencies, voted to ban it from the airwaves. Far from curbing either the hard sell or the presentation of smoking as a "pleasant and satisfying habit enjoyed by healthy and attractive people," TV carried $230 million of smoking ads in 1967, an increase over the amount spent in 1964, $170 million.

Yet the cardinal sin, the FTC concluded, was the Tobacco Institutes' tactic of planting pro-smoking stories in such magazines as *True* which played down the link between smoking and cancer. The stories were written by Hill and Knowlton, a public relations firm, and distributed by Tiderock Corporation, a New York promotion company, headed by former Ted Bates & Company president Rosser Reeves. One of their top accounts was the Tobacco Institute.

The cigarette advertising issue will be debated for years. It's a vastly complicated problem. Unlike most consumer issues choice does exist in the marketplace; people know by now what smoking does to lungs. But the advertising industry can reduce the hostility welling up around the issue by taking a step toward de-escalation. One possibility has been proposed by Senator Warren Magnuson and the late Robert Kennedy: limiting smoking ads to television hours after ten p.m. Another approach would have the networks provide equal time for anti-smoking commercials.

What must change, asserts Federal Trade Commission member Mary Gardiner Jones, is not so much the practices but the attitudes of advertising men. The self-awareness and self-assertiveness the consumer is exhibiting in the marketplace, she has said, "does not reflect any overall disenchantment with our free enterprise system or with American business as a whole. Consumers are fully aware of its innovative genius. Rather it is reflective of his desire to be treated as a mature individual."

Some advertising men appreciate Miss Jones' views and even agree with them but the system that has proved so profitable and successful probably can never be changed. It is too rigid and inflexible. Few understand better than J. Walter Thompson Chairman Strouse. "It would be easy," he said in 1968, "for those in advertising to assume a holier-than-thou attitude toward the constant violation of truthfulness and good taste in many other aspects of our American life—the political scene, in the entertainment world, among the demonstrators and riot leaders on our city streets and on our campuses. But we must not be complacent or indulge in self congratulations. As ours is the most public kind of responsibility, more is demanded of us than others. And we have more to give. . .we are all of us imperfect in our understanding, sometimes in our objectives, more often in our action. We should be determined to do our best within the moral and ethical environment of our times—and who can ask for more than that?"

Danger

chapter 7

For decades most American consumers have blithely assumed that the undiminished array of products, gadgets and gimcracks flooding into the marketplace furnished quality, utility, safety and a touch of status and fashion to boot. No one seriously questioned the right of industry to make a profit, for profit is the fuel of progress, but industry put gratification of the consumer's needs first. Didn't advertisements constantly reinforce that soothing assumption?

Unhappily for the housewife's idealized conception of corporate motives, fed by a potpourri of puffery from women's magazines, that assessment, while still intact, is now tattered and no longer can be left totally unchallenged; evidence that shakes a once sacrosanct presumption is too overwhelming.

Describing the scene in a 1966 report, the White House Consumer Advisory Council arrived at the conclusion that the marketplace is marked by "much confusion, ignorance, some deception and even fraud, where in fact, understanding and honesty ideally should prevail."

In the next two years, the most vigorous consumer protection period in congressional history, a rich vein of unacceptably grim detail was unearthed in such established industries as meat, tires, appliances, gas pipelines, drugs, fish and poultry. Surveying the arena in 1968, a high White House official added another dimension to the 1966 report: "There is a great deal of danger, too."

At least 250,000 potentially hazardous consumer products are present on the market today, an average of 45 per household.

The dangers they represent exclude the health hazards that exist
in too many drugs and a surprising amount of meat. Moreover,
the National Safety Council predicts that at least 60,000
Americans will be killed in 1968 in nonhighway accidents;
another ten million will suffer disabling injuries. Products, to be
sure, are not always the killers but in far too many cases they are,
consumer leaders assert. The fact remains that despite such health
problems as cancer and heart disease, the major cause of death for
people between one and 36 years old is an accident.

Upon signing the Flammable Fabrics Act in 1967, President
Johnson told an audience in the East Room: "Our society is
more prosperous and it's more complex than any the world has
ever known. It has not altogether eliminated some of these
avoidable dangers." Lyndon Johnson has not been known for his
understatements but he made one there.

In 1967, Senator Warren Magnuson and his energetic
Commerce Committee together with Consumers Union assembled
a ten-year glossary of dangerous and hazardous products. For
those who want to remain confident of U.S. industry's innovative
abilities, the results were not very reassuring. Some radio and
television sets were so shoddily assembled that enough current
escaped to give the viewer a jolting shock. Dangerously exposed
electrical terminals were found to exist on large numbers of
kitchen ranges, broilers, portable heaters and dehumidifiers.
Other dangers existed, the study determined, in such common
products of the good life as garbage disposals, garden sprayers,
travel irons and childrens' toys with metal edges sharp enough to
cut. Consumers Union's conclusion: 376 products were rated not
acceptable for use. But for many the real shocker was delivered
by Senator Magnuson when he said after the study that "these
products were not confined to fly-by-night firms; some came
from the most reputable manufacturers in the country."

No one is precisely certain of the number of hazardous
products marketed every year, but there is ample evidence
nevertheless of Magnuson's thesis—and the heart of Ralph Nader's
consumer doctrine—that fly-by-night practices exist at the very
core of the U.S. corporate community.

As television set manufacturers prepared for the coming
color boom in 1966 quality control slipped badly. One result:
General Electric built and sold at least 90,000 large screen sets

which emitted excessive x-rays through the bottoms of the sets. Some of the sets, before they were recalled, discharged 50,000 milliroentgens an hour, 100,000 times the level determined as safe by the National Council on Radiation Protection.

One sensitive outpost of danger prevention is Underwriters Laboratories in Chicago. Many large companies submit their products for testing before they are sold but since U.L. flunks 50 per cent of the candidates, many others don't bother. They market them anyway. "Hardly a day goes by," reports Senator Magnuson, "when I and my staff do not hear of a new hazardous product."

Sometimes the major companies which provide crucial ingredients for a product don't realize, or properly insure against, the possibility that the final product might be hazardous. A startling example is the case of X-33 water repellent manufactured for waterproofing cellars and houses by the Wilmington Chemical Corporation. One ingredient: a DuPont chemical named Tyzor HS. While DuPont didn't manufacture or market the final product, mostly composed of a Shell Oil Company solvent, Wilmington Chemical Corporation was granted permission by DuPont to advertise its product with the DuPont name. After a series of deaths and injuries caused by flash explosions, the Federal Trade Commission wheeled up, ruling that X-33 not only didn't measure up to the claims Wilmington Chemical ascribed to it but was dangerous. Neither of the companies had ever tested X-33 to determine whether its utility matched the claims on the label.

But on other occasions manufacturers know exactly what they are doing. *Electric Appliance Service News*, quoting Earl Holst, president of the National Appliance and Radio-TV Dealers Association recently reported: "Mr. Holst. . .on a visit to the production line of a particular manufacturer pointed to a new product and said, 'The first three of those we received didn't work.' He was told that the factory already knew about this, but shipped them anyway, figuring it was cheaper to repair them in the field. . ." Others wonder what the circumstances were in Detroit in the 1963 model year when, after purchasing and testing 32 autos, Consumers Union testers experienced repairs and breakdowns on all but one before 2000 miles had been driven.

If there is any single reason why Senators and Representatives have moved toward support of consumer legislation it is that the gap between appearance and reality in the marketplace, as personified by dangerous products, is wide enough to embarrass them into action. It is a picture contrary to the image of America they like and few of them are anxious to appear in the role of widening that gap through inaction.

If the consumerists are correct then the real world, as Ralph Nader insists, is one in which "people are being killed, injured and inconvenienced by the products and processes of technology." Nader, for his part, carries that assessment to the extreme. "As long as there is undue and parochial attention paid to the short range economic utility of product and process at the same time that the short and long range biological consequences are treated with indifference or contempt, our society is going to plunge into deeper collective cruelties."

Nader is not exaggerating. Acknowledging that human error and carelessness are involved, the scene is nevertheless grotesque, and much of it is avoidable. According to the National Safety Council, at least 175,000 people are mangled yearly by power lawn mowers; faulty electronic products electrocute 1,000 others; at least 175,000 suffer severe burns, and 12,000 die from incendiary clothing and upholstery. As shocking as any of that may be, 2,000 people are accidently poisoned every year, 25 per cent under five years old because of improper labeling or nonlabeling. The killers are common, everyday household products, from soap to aspirin and insecticide to detergent. And, the consumerists ask, how is it that American industry, which has the expertise and finesse to send a high-performance, microminiaturized space ship to Mars, can't master the technology of constructing glass doors that don't maim or kill 100,000 people a year?

The picture, however, is not entirely depressing. The future is, in fact, hopeful now that the bodily rights of consumers are being recognized. A fundamental, qualitative change is needed, proclaim the consumerists, not just in the quality control of products but in the attitude of the manufacturers. Though they were unnecessarily contentious at times, the auto safety hearings and the meat debates did serve another purpose, besides insuring that consumers would be better protected: they illuminated the little known fact that not only do small, disreputable companies occasionally work against the consumer's interests but so do powerful, well known blue chip companies, such as Armour, Swift, and General Motors. Exposure and the resulting embarrassment, in short, were needed.

Among the most notable efforts bringing on a change is the White House Commission on Product Safety, authorized by President Johnson in 1967. It is conducting a two-year study of the categories of household products which present an unreasonable risk of injury to the consuming public. It will also determine the extent to which industry self-regulation, judicial decisions on product liability, and local, state and federal statutes are adequate to protect buyers against dangerous products. In Johnson's words, the Commission's purpose is to "stop tragedy before tragedy strikes." Later, while rallying a small group of Congressmen at the White House to support his bills, he warned: "You better get with it. People are tired of meat with worms in it, blouses that burn and pipelines that blow up under their homes."

They are and that fact, along with pressure from the White House to respond with reform, has not been lost on Washington lobbyists. In their weekly intelligence cables, they've been warning their board chairmen that the new climate is: seller beware.

Consider, for example, the radical shift in viewpoint within just one company, Bristol-Myers, a leading pharmaceutical house. Back in 1940, when the consumer protectionists of the New Deal years were breathing their last, company president William Bristol told an industry audience, "I don't know how many of you are aware of the consumer movement so-called. There are 27 publications and organizations such as Consumers Research and Consumers Union feeding John Henry Public a lot of unsubstantiated and unsubstantiable so-called facts. It's grand reading, good fiction and unfortunately it is growing and undermining our industry. Courses are given in schools and universities along the same line. It's a constant gunfire on our business, on our jobs. . .I don't think we can fight it singlehanded, but I do think we can do our share."

For more than 20 years he did. at least until his brother Lee, a vice-president, offered an entirely different appraisal of the

consumer scene in a speech to New York's Sales Executive Club:
"The great American ailment is manifest on all sides by a
deepening shade in our ethics (both business and social), a
sloppiness in our services, a mediocrity in our manufacture and a
growing distrust and even anger in the public's mind."

These days the first Bristol would have trouble scaring up
an audience, at least one composed of anyone who has read
congressional testimony in the past few years. Congressmen and
consumerists alike now trumpet a new theme, and businessmen
are beginning to pick up the tempo. The time has arrived in
America to deal with the social costs of private enterprise, which
by definition means reducing the painful, dangerous by-products
of great engineering accomplishments, whether air and water
polution, contamination of soil and food or the hazards of autos,
drugs and appliances. And now is also the time to deal with what
Ralph Nader terms, "the attitudes, conditions and disincentives
which have prevented a comprehensive development of remedial
engineering to reduce markedly the social costs of private
enterprise." There is nothing inevitable, for example, about
highway accidents, as the nation has discovered since the safety
law went on the books.

Detroit and Safety

Wheeling down a Michigan road in early 1968, a 55-year-old
man driving a 1967 model car collided with another car, head on
at 50 miles per hour. Not only did the man survive an apparently
unsurvivable crash, but he escaped with relatively minor injuries:
bruised legs and stomach and a broken nose. If he'd been driving
a model built before 1967, before the Federal Traffic Safety Act,
the chances would have been better than even that he would have
been killed. The difference: an energy absorbing steering column
which, despite the big four's early opposition, is now required on
all cars built in and after 1967.

In another example, the driver of a pre-safety bill compact
car, who wasn't wearing a seat belt, suffered severe neck and chin
cuts, a number of broken ribs, internal injuries and a broken leg
when his car smashed into a 1967 model at 35 miles per hour.
Seven months after the accident, the imprint of the horn button
was still visible on his chest. The driver of the other car? He

suffered minor injuries but was not hospitalized. His steering
column had compressed more than four inches.

After decades of assigning highway deaths to the classic
"nut behind the wheel" both industry and the government have
begun to construct a far more rigorous framework of responsibility for reducing, if not ending, highway casualties which kill
more people than all wars combined. "Fundamental to the
emergence of this national policy on motor vehicle safety," says
archcritic Nader, "is the recognition of a value and a capability."
The value is the right of people not to have their physical
integrity violated by hazardous autos—whether by product design
or by construction. The capability, of course, is an engineering
one, the capability to invent the technological future once the
nation decides that it wants the rich benefits of such a future.

If there was an impetus for auto safety reform, apart from
the General Motors private detective affair, it was the result of a
powerful meshing of deeply felt values and eminently graspable
remedies. So much of the carnage is avoidable if products can be
made to forgive the way a 2,000 miles per hour fighter plane or a
space ship does. The difference, of course, is that in the
companies which make space ships and secret reconnaissance
aircraft, engineers and safety experts don't wallow in the
middle-management mud, playing third alto to higher-ranking
stylists and marketing men.

The shift in the Federal government's approach to highway
safety and the impact that approach is having has rarely been
illustrated better than by Federal Highway Administrator Lowell
Bridwell during his department's appropriation hearings on
Capitol Hill in April 1968.

While being questioned by Representative Charles Jonas of
North Carolina, the following exchange occurred.

> *Jonas:* I don't see how you can justify any expanded
> safety program unless you know where your problem is.
> Shouldn't the first step be to identify the cause of these acci-
> dents and see what the point is at which we should be direct-
> ing our attention. . .?
> *Bridwell:* Mr. Jonas, I agree that that is a correct point
> of view. . .our problem in highway safety in general is that the
> cause of accidents has been very largely in the past left to the
> police investigation and their investigations have concentrated

almost entirely upon pinpointing the so-called guilty party
and don't get to the cause, but only at the problem of liability.

Jonas: From your investigations and the study you have
given to the subject, would you agree that it is a fair statement
that by far the greater number of accidents, the greatest cause
of accidents is reckless and careless driving by individuals?

Bridwell: I don't believe I could make that statement,
Mr. Jonas.

Speed and careless drivers cause accidents, of that there is
no question. But cars kill. As government research is now
beginning to show, spectacular accidents get the widest, splashiest
publicity but they account for only a small minority of the
53,000 highway deaths a year. A study made in California in
1967, for example, revealed that after a large sampling of
accident wreckage was sifted and examined, mechanical failure
was a direct cause in 20 per cent of the crashes. It's no wonder
that between 1966 when the Traffic Safety Bill passed and
December 1967, the big four manufacturers pulled back five
million cars to check for possible mechanical defects, one half of
the total production run that year.

In its research, the National Highway Safety Bureau is
employing the total systems approach to reduce accidents. Most
accidents, for example, involve more factors than just the driver.
In a series of interactions the vehicle, the road and the driver set
up the chain of events that culminates in accidents. Driving too
fast may create no problem, but driving too fast at night in a car
with poor lights on a winding road could result in the car
careening off the road into a ditch. Correcting any one of these
factors—straightening the road, improving the lighting, or slower
driving—probably would prevent the accident. Simple as this
seems, the government began the total approach only in this
decade.

One of the Safety Bureau's projects is developing an
electronic route guidance system. It works this way. As the driver
approaches an intersection, a dashboard device signals the driver
whether he should turn left or right or go straight ahead. Traffic
flow would be increased and make for safer operation. There is
also on the drawing boards a flow-sensing surveillance system.
Television cameras mounted at busy urban intersections could
scan the intersection, taping traffic flow, erasing itself auto-

matically and re-exposing for 20 second periods. If an accident occurred, the noise or some other factor would trigger the camera. Investigators could study the tape for hours for clues which might lead to preventive devices.

Until a few years ago traffic safety beliefs have been based on little more than a consensus of subjective judgments, according to Dr. William Haddon, Highway Safety Bureau Director, who has led government programs into new areas of crash prevention, crash survival, and post-crash salvage of the injured and dying. To date, Haddon has issued 30 new safety standards covering 100 specific aspects of vehicle and tire safety performance; 40 others are in preparation in Haddon's office.

Some of the standards include better lighting, defrosting and defogging equipment and better tire performance; standards requiring energy-absorbing steering assemblies that act as a fire net for the driver's chest rather than as a spear, and laminated windshield glass that reduces the severity of injuries; a standard limiting fuel tank rupture and fuel spillage increases the chance for escape and removal of the injured after an accident.

One of Haddon's most interesting developments is an anti-theft device for all cars by 1970. A system is being developed whereby the steering mechanism and the transmission can be locked, reducing the possibility of theft to zero. This is important because at least 100,000 stolen cars crash every year, a rate 200 times that of other cars.

Haddon's research for future standards includes better windshield mounting to prevent crash dislodgment; strengthening the side structure of cars to reduce frequent deaths and injuries happening daily in intersection and other lateral impacts. A well placed company executive admitted to him a few months ago: "We were appalled when we tested our own cars to discover they gave us no protection from side impact." Fresh from that shock, the industry is now driving ahead of the government safety group, developing lifesaving side structure supports for future model runs, even before Dr. Haddon has proposed a standard. If other industry leaders begin reacting with such progressive programs, Ralph Nader will be out of work. The companies in Detroit, whatever their motives, were plainly horrified at the road tests. For even at low speeds, around 30 miles per hour, the impacting

car penetrates as far as the steering wheel on current models; in a
right side collision, the right side often will be pushed as far as the
driver, crushing all the passengers.

Some Congressmen can contest the cost of the government's
traffic safety program but at $25,000 per standard, the invest-
ment is a remarkably good one. Any effort, in fact, which offers
potential for reducing the incredible economic damage of
highway accidents ($30 million a day) and human loss is worth
the cost. Each week 70,000 Americans are injured and 1,000
killed. On an annual basis that equals the total American battle
losses in 3 years of the Korean War.

Budgetary arguments are inevitable, but already Dr. Haddon
has reported a payoff in human lives. Highway injuries decreased
400,000 in the first year of the safety program, a dramatic 10 per
cent drop despite a rise in auto registrations.

A framework for a viable safety program has been
constructed and should continue to expand now that the
industry's early opposition has dwindled and even been replaced
to some extent by a cooperative attitude. One can only mourn
for the 300,000 drivers who have been speared to death in the
past 40 years because their cars lacked energy absorbing steering
columns. If the manufacturers had chosen to save those lives, the
know-how was there for the task. It was the will that was missing.
If someone had begun asking questions when the first Model T's
rattled down the roads about what was killing drivers, they would
have discovered that the steering shaft was a solid piece of steel,
from the front end of the car to the driver's chest.

Safe Tires

For all the soothing advertising about safety rushing from
the nation's major tire manufacturers, investigations by Senator
Gaylord Nelson and the Federal Trade Commission indicate that
the tires on many new autos are inadequate to handle maximum
loads. What's more, some original equipment tires can't be
operated safely at the speeds the vehicles are capable of achieving.
In fact, the consumer is provided precious little information
about some very vital criteria, including a tire's impact resistance,
endurance, traction, and mileage.

In the spring of 1968, Nelson's senate office was inundated with complaints from buyers about Firestone Wide Oval Tires. The tires not only showed unusually rapid tread wear, the complaints said, but the sidewalls had cracked and split.

Nelson set his staff to work. "I was shocked to discover how readily tire industry sources confirmed these reports," he said later, "about trouble with the Wide Oval. These people I talked with were well aware of the splitting and cracking as well as the unusually rapid tread wear and some other deficiencies."

Only after he was sure that Firestone hadn't ordered the defective tires recalled, did he confront the company. Privately, officials conceded that the letter writers had scored a point. There were problems with the Wide Ovals. Nelson found it astonishing that a large, respected company "privately concedes that it had produced a defective product, yet refuses publicly to take responsibility for the recall of that product."

Unquestionably, Firestone drew much of the fire down on its own position. The Nelson episode occurred amidst the company's spring advertising campaign. It's theme: "When you buy a Firestone tire no matter how much or how little you pay, you get a safe tire."

To one California tire dealer, who trafficked in Firestone products, that ad was the limit. "I am prepared to testify under oath," he wrote Nelson, "that I have seen many, many Firestone Wide Ovals with both small and large separations and cracks. These were all defects of a very serious nature. . .all the tire dealers I know have had similar experiences with Wide Ovals." When the time-consuming fracas was over, Firestone recalled the defective tires and made the necessary changes in the manufacturing process.

Complaints from consumers about poor quality and deceptive pricing had been gathering moss in Washington for years, until this decade when the Federal Trade Commission and Congress decided to investigate their merits, despite some strong words of discouragement from tire industry officials. "It wasn't pretty," a key Senator recalls. Apart from the incredible number and variety of brands available, at least 1,100 from coast to coast, the probers found that consumers basically had no way of determining for themselves what such words as "deluxe," "first line," "premium" and "super deluxe" meant to them. As consumer expert Sidney Margolius has written, "each manufacturer could call a tire anything he wanted to, and apparently did. Sometimes a manufacturer would call a mediocre grade 'super,' and a second grade, 'deluxe'."

The industry's first line of defense was to press for a system of voluntary standards. That was hardly a breakthrough since the common denominator was so low that most, if not all, tires could meet the standards. Subsequently, Congress authorized the Commerce Department to establish a series of safety and grading standards, the first government-developed guidelines for product quality outside the food area. When the grading standards are implemented, the consumer will know what he is buying to a degree as yet unequalled. If he doesn't care much about quality, which has been the argument industries have frequently used to head off standards and consumer protection regulation, that's his privilege. But many consumers do care, if the thousands of letters cascading into Washington are any guide, and it is to end the tire-buying nightmare that the Commerce Department has taken action.

The Federal Trade Commission, for its part, has promulgated some effective tire advertising guides. Under a 1967 ruling, tire manufacturers were obligated to provide buyers with information that enables him to match the weight of his car with the performance of the hundreds of possible choices available. The consumer leaders, however, haven't hung their lances on the wall; much more disclosure should be made mandatory, they say, before the tire buyer and the tire seller can meet on a level that even approaches equal terms.

Industry critics direct their fiercest tirade at the suppression of innovation within the industry, the reluctance to advance the state of the art for the buyer's benefit. Ted Rowse, editor of Washington's best consumer newsletter, *U.S. Consumer*, insists that back in 1957, Firestone developed but never marketed a tubeless tire equipped with a special valve for receiving injections of linseed oil. Oxygen is a natural enemy of tire life because it damages rubber. Linseed oil nearly eliminates the oxidation process by absorbing oxygen, leaving only nitrogen inside the tire. Manufacturers have long known that nitrogen can lengthen a tire's life but for one reason or another, few consumers have enjoyed the benefits of the breakthrough.

There has been a breakthrough, however, as research by one Texas company, Three-T-Fleet of El Paso, reveals. Tire life was increased at least 25 per cent and as much as 50 per cent after extensive nitrogen treatment. Such advantages are not available to the consumer, unless he wants to do it himself, and yet the manufacturers' band plays on about quality control excellence and innovation.

Consumer Reports in 1968 summed up the conditions in the rubber jungle, through which the buyer must hack his way if he wants a safe, fairly priced tire: "You can't consistently count on any single type of tire or material to give better performance than another." Moreover, while the buyer waits for reform he must make his decision from the broadest spectrum imaginable, tread life ranging from 15,000 to 40,000 miles, costs per 10,000 miles of driving on a full set of $40 to $130.

If the industry can't produce safe tires the consumerists petition for the next best break. The industry advertising should be toned down so that buyers aren't misled into believing they are driving on miracle tires.

There has been movement toward reform, but, unhappily, the conclusions of the Consumer Advisory Council are nearly as relevant today as they were in 1966. "It is a sad commentary that, as a cost-cutting device, inferior grades of tires are provided on many new cars. There is no defense for an automaker equipping new cars with tires that are not capable of safely carrying a full load of passengers under all conditions commonly encountered...even the one point about which the consumer feels sure, the size of the tire he needs, presents an element of uncertainty: whether in fact he gets that size...a serious hazard results when the consumer calculates the load capacity of his car on the basis of the tire size he requested but is riding on a smaller tire."

Dangerous Drugs

In few other areas of the U.S. marketplace is the consumer as uninformed as he is when he buys drugs prescribed for him by his doctors, or for that matter, when he buys any kind of health remedies. Americans, the most health conscious population in history, consume mountains of pills, bromides, drugs and palliatives on doctors' orders. The doctors' information to a large extent comes from the drug industry's detail men, a euphemism for salesmen. Standing between them and millions of Americans is the Food and Drug Administration, whose vigilance varies. At the very least, the Consumer Advisory Council study warned, "the patient who receives a prescription from his physician should have reasonable confidence and expectation that the drug is truly needed."

The Kefauver drug hearings of the early 1960s provided new insights for those consumers who may have wanted to know more about the behind-the-scenes operations of the drugmakers. What was revealed was a picture of internal struggling between research men anxious to conduct thorough tests and the marketing men, whose eyes were trained on the sales and profit charts.

The hearings produced enough evidence to warrant new congressional authority over the industry, including stiffer testing programs for industry before a drug could be approved by the FDA for sale. A host of questionable drugs have been held off the market until their efficacy has been established thanks to Senator Kefauver's efforts.

There were other new requirements established by Kefauver's bill, such as a review of 3,600 pharmaceutical products marketed between 1938 and 1962. Designated to conduct the review was a team of professionals from the National Academy of Sciences—National Research Council. The conclusions reportedly reached by the review team are guaranteed to place the drugmakers on the defensive more than Kefauver ever did, if that is possible. Only about ten per cent of the drug products marketed between 1938 and 1962 wholly measure up to the claims made for them; at least another ten per cent should be thrown off the market because they have no value one way or another.

Whether these findings will have an impact on the industry is dubious, the consumer leaders reason. If the new Kefauver amendments are a guide, however, the economic impact will be hardly noticeable. Though the drugmakers complained that the 1962 amendments would disrupt the inexorably rising profit and sales indicators, the industry's rate of return on net worth, 18 per cent, still leads all U.S. industries while profit return on sales has actually increased since the new legislation, from 9.8 per cent to 10.7 per cent, according to *Fortune* magazine.

Then as now, the consumer suffers not only from physical malady but also from a woeful lack of relevant information about the drugs he takes. His only sources currently are exchanges between his doctor and the drugmakers' detail men who daily bombard doctors and druggists with new pills and antibiotics, accompanied by extravagant claims as to their potency and utility. Rarely, if ever, does news of a particular drug's disadvantages filter through that maze of overstatements.

The consumerists are fond of tracing the case of Chloromycetin, a broad spectrum antibiotic which was introduced by Parke, Davis in 1949, as an illustration of the occasional imbalances between sales and safety. If the drug business is a delicate balancing act between costs, profits and benefits to the patients, most consumerists believe that in the case of Chloromycetin, the scale tipped too far toward sales.

Soon after Parke, Davis had begun selling the drug, evidence cropped up that serious side-effects sometimes accompanied the cure. A sample: blood poisoning and aplastic anemia. It was held that the antibiotic was appropriate for typhoid conditions and for patients with Rocky Mountain spotted fever but wider use for such common ailments as respiratory infections and colds was risky. Looking on with dismay as four million people in 1960 alone were given Chloromycetin, such watchdogs as Senator Gaylord Nelson and Morton Mintz of *The Washington Post* shuddered. In their view, only a few thousand people who were down with typhoid should be treated with the prescription. Meanwhile, reports of fatalities and severe side effects grew in number.

When Parke, Davis' patent for Chloromycetin expired in 1966 (generic name, chloramphenicol), a half-dozen of the competitors rushed in with their own brands. Rugged though the new competition has been, Parke, Davis still draws a third of its sales and a third of its earnings from Chloromycetin.

Critics of the consumer movement object to excessive emphasis of the case because the pattern is not often repeated. On the other hand, much can be learned from it, not only because so many large, well known firms have been involved; new insights are provided into the world of the detail men.

In the 1950s, James Watkins, 10, of La Canada, California, came down with a urinary tract infection. His harried father, Dr. Albe Watkins, searched the family medicine chest for a cure. He recalled that Parke, Davis detail men, during one of their calls to his office, had touted Chloromycetin as being "perfectly safe." He gave it to his son. Three months later the boy died of aplastic anemia, in agony. "I might have done better," his father told a Senate committee later, "had I taken a gun and shot him."

Regrettably, there are hundreds of recorded cases like that one, even thousands, the morbid result of doctors treating patients for colds and other minor ailments, when other drugs would be demonstrably safer. "Using Chloromycetin for everyday ailments is like shooting a chicken with a bazooka," a government official confided recently. The company, no doubt, has been aware of dangers. Because it is required to, the company has published warnings in American medical journals. And yet, when it advertises in foreign medical journals, where there is no requirement, it doesn't.

During one recent congressional airing of the drug industry's safety problems, some illuminating testimony was given by Dr. William Hewson of West Chester, Pennsylvania. A few months before while wearing his other hat as a lawyer, he won a $215,000 jury award for the estate of Mary Ann Incollinge, a child who died under the same circumstances James Watkins had.

"The great disservice of the detail men is not their exaggeration of a drug's beneficial uses," Dr. Hewson explained, "but in their approach to its toxic effects. Commonly the toxicity is not discussed thoroughly, is played down, and is not even broached. The otherwise informed physician is thereby grossly misled."

As a practicing physician, Dr. Hewson said he didn't recall "the Parke, Davis detail men ever discussing the relationship between administration of the drug and the development of blood dyscrasias. . .Of the many physicians I have talked to with regard to these detailing methods, not one has stated that the Parke, Davis men voluntarily brought the toxicity to the physicians' attention."

Hammering first at high prices, Senator Kefauver in 1962 dug into the allegation that there was profit for drugmakers who could deceive physicians. He must have found evidence, for one of the amendments in the 1962 legislative package included one which requires that "all advertisements and other descriptive matter must carry a true statement in brief summary of efficacy, side effects," and conditions in which the drug should not be used. The FDA was given right of review.

Under that stronger umbrella of prevention, the FDA has since taken 33 formal actions against 26 well known manufacturers, with Abbott Laboratories and Upjohn Company cited three times each. Under pressure from FDA administrator James Goddard, who resigned for a job in private industry July 1, 1968, drug companies have allowed a beam of light to penetrate its interiors. Despite their self-righteous facade, drugmakers do make mistakes. Since February 1967, 21 companies have mailed 23 letters correcting overstatements and softening claims to more than 280,000 doctors across the nation. A sample:

→ FDA stopped shipments of Bristol Laboratories' Dynapen because it exceeded approved labeling by claiming general use when such use might endanger a whole class of those drugs as "reserves" against staphylococci germs. Government officials demanded a correction letter for what was plainly a case of overpromotion.

→ Birth control pill manufacturers played down the hazards of the pills and, under FDA pressure, later told the nation's physicians as much. The products included Mead Johnson's Oracon, Syntex's Norinyl-1 and Norquen, and Searle's Ovulen-21. No one doubts the effectiveness of the pills, but many concerned drug industry watchers want women to know that various hazards accompany fertility control, including nausea, bloating, changes in menstrual flow and occasionally mental depression, breast enlargement, loss of scalp hair and dizziness. The new ads advise that women should stop taking the pills if they experience a sudden partial or complete loss of vision, or if migraine headaches develop.

Other letters include apologies to doctors by Ayerst for implying that a link existed between cholesterol-lowering Atromid-S and a "beneficial effect" on heart disease; by Geigy for a claim "not supported by the data" that Hygroton lowers blood pressure.

Another fascinating look inside the world of the drugmakers' detail men was provided by Tony Clifton in the *Sunday*

Times of London in October 1967. Quoting from a pamphlet distributed in England by Merck & Company, Clifton described some of the instructions given to detail men before they make their rounds. First, "develop eye contact habits that help to signal sincerity. . .look your customer *right in the eye*. . .Keep your sincerity flag of good eye-contact flying." Second, "when the doctor invites you to take a chair, *sit animatedly*." Former E. R. Squibb medical director Dr. A. Dale Console has said that some detail men are driven by the maxim, "if you can't convince them, confuse them."

The era of "seller beware" has not yet arrived for the drugmakers, but it is coming. No drug company deliberately plans to use drug consumers as guinea pigs but in Washington there exists a strong feeling that the consequences are the same as if they did. Extensive testing before marketing is a small price to pay for health and safety, particularly when the industry has the resources. Furthermore, exploitation is no longer a tolerable condition in 20th century America. What separates the drug issue from others in the consumer arena and renders drug consumers more silent is the fact that even though they buy, it is the physicians who order. And so when drug reform is set in motion in Congress, the fullest measure of responsibility rests upon the shoulders of the FDA; the real voice of the drug consumer seldom filters through because he doesn't know what to do. How much of a voice do consumers have? "Very little," commissioner Goddard said when he was sworn in two years ago, "unless it is ours."

In the final analysis, the consumers must rely on the drugmakers' social consciousness. "Thalidomide taught us," Morton Mintz wrote in 1967, "that the unborn child may have the most vital concern with the chemicals ingested by its mother. Yet a fetus is hardly in the best position to file a legal brief with the FDA in hopes of assuring that an advertisement will not mislead a physician into prescribing a needlessly dangerous drug that will cross the placental barrier."

Cleaner Meat, Fish and Chicken

When President Theodore Roosevelt led the first major, successful drive for pure food and drug laws, he was fought at every turn by the food and drug industry. The slaughterhouse conditions might have been abominable, but the companies fought to preserve the right of free choice for themselves and for the consumers' right to be wrong, which in those days included food poisoning. During the height of the hearings in 1906, which were triggered by Upton Sinclair's exposé, *The Evening Post* published a rhyme describing the conditions.

> "Mary had a little lamb
> And when she saw it sicken
> She shipped it off to Packington
> And now it's labeled 'chicken'."

A wave of indignation swept the country again in 1967 when meat plant conditions were publicized. To advocates of reform of the 1960s, the *Evening Post* rhyme was regrettably germane. The 1906 act, by exempting intrastate plants from inspection, had left a loophole wide enough for hundreds of impure meat merchants to drive their trucks through. Before the 1967 meat bill, fully one-quarter of the 50 billion pounds of meat processed in the U.S. was inspected only by the states, whose programs congressional testimony established were tantamount to no inspection at all. Conditions in the poultry industry, if possible, represented even greater health dangers to the consumer. If consumers knew about the conditions, Senator Joseph Montoya of New Mexico told the Senate in August 1968, "they would never pick up another piece of poultry again, except to chuck it out the back door for the vultures." An estimated 11.5 billion pounds of poultry products are produced annually, of which at least 1.5 billion pounds are inspected solely by the states. Only five states have had active inspection programs.

Pressing for a legislative program similar to the meat bill, Senator Montoya cited an Agriculture Department survey made in January 1968, of 97 plants which were not subject to federal inspection. The plants were in Alabama, California, Mississippi, Florida, Ohio, Texas, South and North Carolina, Missouri, and Tennessee. Some poultry and poultry products, said the report, are processed in "repulsive...primitive conditions," including fly and rodent infestation and "unbelievably filthy and stinking" picking rooms and equipment.

Once again, horrible revelations were needed to prod Congress into action. Far more than mere political demagoguery was the lever that propelled new inspection bills through: at least 2 million Americans contract such diseases as botulism and salmonellosis a year from inadequate, diseased food, mostly meat and poultry.

Such consumerists as Senator Walter Mondale and Ralph Nader jolted millions of consumers and Congressmen from their reverie with reports of intolerable processing conditions. A glance at the seamy underside of the free enterprise system was provided by Senator Mondale during the meat debates. There were some 15,000 meat packing plants dealing in meats sold only within states, subject to state and county and municipal laws. "A number of these were generally defective or not enforced for the protection of consumers," he said, while the plants were deliberately established "out of reach of Federal inspection" to effect savings "by passing the sick meat to consumers" and by using "additives not permitted under Federal regulation."

For the first time, consumers were allowed into the world of the "cripple buyers," who deal in "4-D" meat, dead, dying, disabled or diseased animals. Not only were those dealers out of reach of Federal inspectors but state inspectors rarely ventured near them. Reports of bribery were widespread.

Several times during the meat and poultry hearings in 1967 and 1968, meat inspectors were asked whether they would buy such meat for their own families. The answer was always no. Why should anyone else, either? Ultimately, congressional consciences became so aroused that reform legislation was passed, but only with daily pressure from Betty Furness and the White House.

If these bills are properly financed with appropriations so that enough new Federal inspectors can be hired, the consumer will be much less likely to buy dangerous meat and poultry in the future. Top executives in both industries have come to realize the hard way that strict regulation is good business; if consumers have confidence, they'll buy more. As a measure of the consumer movement, the poultry interests recognized the need for reform in 1968 and supported the bill from the beginning. The year before, the meat interests reluctantly came around under pressure from all sides.

The lesson doesn't always get through, however. About six months after President Johnson signed the meat bill, a speech was delivered by William Heimlich, a vice-president of the Association

of Better Business Bureaus International. His topic was consumerism. "We cannot quarrel with the thesis that the government has a right and the duty to protect the health and safety of
the consumer. But we have every right to debate the question of
whether the government can protect the consumer from his own
bad judgment. Freedom of choice is a precious right and much of
the unrest in those countries where government rules the
marketplace with an iron hand is directly traceable to the
demands of the people for the right of free choice." Mr. Heimlich
evidently missed the message of the meat bill. Free choice of
rotten meat and poultry is no longer tolerated by the leaders of
the consumer movement and their followers.

The disclosures jarred enough Americans so that they took
refuge in eating fish; all food wasn't hazardous, was it? There is
no industry, with the exception of lumbering that has been on the
American scene longer than fishing. But there is strong evidence
that as in the meat and poultry industries, there is as much
money to be made in the commercial market with bad fish as
with good fish. "Many ships in the commercial fleet are old and
unsanitary," Ralph Nader has written in the *New Republic*. "But
even the more modern portions of the domestic fishing fleet have
yet to surmount the long time that elapses between the fish catch
and its processing. Dead fish often rest 5 to 14 days in the hold
pens with ice piled on top of them. The unique odors attendant
upon decomposition aboard ship proliferate here. Deficient
temperature control is the most serious problem. Storage at
temperatures above the level of $0°$ F bring deteriorating havoc on
this highly perishable commodity."

A Consumers Union study revealed the dangerous whirlwind
the housewife can reap from fish products; 85 per cent of 646
cans of salmon (51 brands) were on the verge of discoloration and
mushiness; 98 samples of 120 samples of frozen raw breaded
shrimp tested contained coagulase positive staphylococci; 55
samples of 120 samples of cod, haddock and ocean perch fillets
were of substandard quality.

There is ample evidence that housewives didn't need such
disclosures to warn them of the possible hazards of bad fish,
imported or domestic. Fish sales have not grown at all in the last
20 years and per capita consumption, 11 pounds a year, is
approximately the same as it was in 1948.

All the housewife needs is to hear more reports of poisoning and she'll switch to another menu. Tuna sales, for example, dropped sharply in May 1966 after 400 cases of salmonella poisoning in New York City were tracked to smoked fish processed in substandard plants. Three years earlier, nine people died from botulism poisoning after eating canned tuna.

The FDA has sought to pressure the industry to take remedial steps. But the industry is shunning the warnings so far. They think disclosure such as Nader's are bad for business, and they are correct.

Early in 1968, W. B. Rankin, a deputy commissioner of the FDA, was scheduled to address a group of fishing industry executives. But at the last minute, his appearance was cancelled. A copy of his speech had fallen into outside hands. Part of it described the results of FDA surveys conducted at several processing plants:

"The fish were hung on wooden sticks for the processing operation. The sticks were encrusted with rotten fish scales and particles from previous batches. Debris from previous batches of fish was trapped in the nicked table top since no attempt was made to clean and sanitize the table between operations. These residues served to contaminate all batches of fish that passed over the table. No attempt was made to clean the rusty wire dip nets that were used to remove the fish from the thawing and brining casks. The nets had buildups of bits of rotten fish flesh and entrails. . .a rusty perforated metal scoop was generally used to mix the brine solutions. In one instance, an employee picked a stick off the floor and used it to mix the brine. . .after smoking, the fish were allowed to stand at room temperature for approximately 4½ hours before they were placed in a refrigerator."

Dangers in the marketplace are proving more extensive than housewives—or their husbands—realize. Unlike air and water pollution, however, remedies for removing them are clearly within reach. There has been a reawakening at Federal, State and local levels; almost daily U.S. industry is being reminded that what is good for the public is also good for business. If some businessmen remain unconvinced, the chances are better than they've ever been in the nation's history that the long arm of consumerism will reach out and remind them of their forgotten responsibilities. Not just the meat, drug, poultry and auto makers have learned that the hard way. So have the men who operate natural gas pipelines, sell medical devices and cosmetics, or pump undue amounts of powerful pesticides into the land and rivers. "To view past, present and future actions as 'anti-business' or as a 'bleeding hearts campaign'," Betty Furness has said, "is to miss the whole point—we have a consumer revolution on our hands—as dynamic a force as the emerging labor movement of the 1930s."

It is, after all, not the consumer who fixes prices or processes diseased meat. Nor is it the consumer, Betty Furness explained to a meeting of the American Trial Lawyers Association in July 1968, who seeks "to undermine business or destroy competition. He is only guilty of the desire to buy wisely and the desire to be assisted through some pertinent information about his purchase. . .he also harbors the not unreasonable desire for some kind of standards and quality controls so that he can compare products wisely. These goals we want to achieve are as American as the 4th of July."

Achieving these goals is no longer a fit subject for academic discussion or abstract postulation, not when the National Commission on Product Safety is running out of file space because so many cases are coming to its attention. Here are some sample cases:

• A 16-month-old boy took the legs off a doll, exposing three-inch spikes, described by his mother as a "lethal weapon."

• A 13-month-old boy hanged himself in his crib with the string of a musical toy designed to entertain babies.

• A woman in New York City wrote, "The plastic lid of my gift coffeemaker caught fire. . .the flame reached almost to the ceiling."

• "For the third time this year my son has had a severe fall from his swing set," wrote a woman from Garland, Texas, "all because the hooks attached to the swing seats last only five days and chains last only about six months."

• A 62-year-old woman in California was standing in a puddle when her electric edger clipped its cord. She was electrocuted.

While not a landmark on the order of the auto safety or meat bill, the 1967 amendments to the Flammable Fabrics Act, nevertheless, extend new protection to buyers of carpets, drapes, hats, gloves and upholstery fabrics. It took 14 years for the bill's basic loophole to be closed; only with wearing apparel did the government have the right to set limits of flammability. A disproportionate number of victims of such perilous products are children or the aged; 1,500 people die from clothing burns annually, another 100,000 are injured.

There is action on many other fronts, as well, protecting consumers against dangerous x-ray machines, toxic food additives, unsafe cosmetics and even sun tan lotion.

Some experts believe that less danger exists in the marketplace today than was present 50 years ago, although the majority view holds that there is substantially more now than ever before. The consumer's sense of rising expectations is demanding that industry do better because it knows how, if it chooses. Should reform not come from within, then the government will be forced to take even more action, a confrontation no one wants, especially understaffed government agencies who already have their hands full.

There are many optimistic indications that business will heed the new watchwords. Furthermore, attacks on the consumer movement are dwindling. There were few, if any, concurring voices when Dr. Oscar Sussman, a vice president of the New Jersey Public Health Association, wrote in the May 1968 issue of *Nation's Business* that the Wholesale Meat Act of 1967 was a "fraud," or that Betty Furness and Ralph Nader were "two self-styled protectors of the public weal (who) are the best known on the bandwagon of mob psychologists and public relations experts who clobbered the meat industry."

What the consumer really wants these days is assurance that the product he buys has integrity. Industry's opposition to such desires accomplishes nothing more than confirming the consumer's worst fears: dangerous imperfections are present in the marketplace.

Deception

chapter 8

In July 1968, Richard von Schilling, 24, a law enforcement officer in Hampton, Virginia received from the local agent of North American Van Lines a cost estimate for moving a standard-sized sofa from Chevy Chase, Maryland to Hampton, a distance of approximately 225 miles. The estimate given was $37.50. Nothing was mentioned about the manner of payment. Late one Sunday afternoon, many weeks later, the moving van arrived, but there was a hitch: before he would unload the sofa, the driver demanded $61.25 in cash or certified check. Otherwise he would be forced to put the piece in storage and add the costs to the bill. If the von Schillings wanted the sofa, in short, they had to pay the ballooned bill. There was no other choice.

"The salesman knocked on my door," Mrs. Louise Cotton of Washington, D. C., told the Senate Commerce Committee on March 7, 1968. "He told me he was selling mattresses that would cause my husband to sleep better at night. He explained that he'd been to hospitals to adjust mattresses for patients, and that if anything happened to my husband like a broken hip or something, he would be able to adjust the mattress to suit his needs. He said the cost would be $212 or $11 a month." Several days afterwards, a credit company mailed Mrs. Cotton a coupon book. It contained some alarming news. She owed a whopping $319.76 for the $212 mattress.

An authoritative inspection of 300 lumber yards, 96 trucks, 49 private dwellings and 272 housing developments not long ago in New Jersey, New York, Pennsylvania and Virginia produced enough detail to fill a state inspector's 55-page transcript. There were many cases, the report said, of "misgrading, mismarking, fraud and the sale of one grade and species and delivery of another." The practice of mixing stamped lumber of one grade with unstamped lumber of a lower grade, still another inspector found, was "so widespread as to properly be called a common trade practice." Simultaneously, the Federal Trade Commission finally pressured the lumber industry into admitting that very little 2 by 4 lumber has been produced in years; mostly it has been 1-7/8 by 3-7/8.

These are only three among thousands of like tales of deception that occur daily in a marketplace jammed with products and services that didn't even exist a few years ago. They have been put there by manufacturers and ad agency brainstormers whose livelihood depends on their ability to psychoanalyze the consumer from the top of his head to the tip of his toes. Their efforts deceive the buyer, whether he knows it or not, in ways far deadlier than past generations have been hoodwinked. Betty Furness recently suggested that much of the deception is in keeping with the old racket in England for which a special decree was issued hundreds of years ago, prohibiting merchants from setting up red or black cloths as shields that concealed from the buyer the bad cloth underneath. Says Miss Furness: "Since we are still struggling with the same thing today, it makes me wonder just how much real progress we have made all these years. . .The intent in too many cases hasn't changed one bit."

Unquestionably, there has been progress over the years, but consumerists believe that the gap between what is tolerated by too many consumers and what is possible is abominably wide. Wherever the consumer turns these days, he finds deception, from drugs to door-to-door sales gimmicks, household moving firms, home improvement plans, and tires, gasoline, warranties, lumber, and even when he buys such everyday staples as bread and orange juice.

"There is a decided tendency in business to use the words 'legal' and 'honest' interchangeably," renegade advertising man E.B. Weiss has written. "When a marketing man says that most businessmen are honest, he really means that most businessmen operate within the law."

Few executives, even privately, accept that scathing appraisal. Most of them agree with Professor James Lorie of the University of Chicago, who says that businessmen are the consumer's true friends, while government regulators and consumerists are his natural enemies.

To most housewives such an argument is lofty and meaningless; high-flown rhetoric doesn't help guide her through the daily wonderland of shopping. Deception portends more serious problems to the housewife than the health hazards of a cereal-packed, waterlogged hot dog. There are economic consequences, too; like a parasite, deception eats away at the family budget, until the consumer begins to wonder where the money went.

The money often goes for a brand-name clear instant chicken soup, a pleasant enough mixture, totally lacking in chicken; or for breakfast juices and juice drinks labeled with promises of nutritional equivalents to fresh orange juice, when in fact, the majority are little more than vitamin packed sugar water. According to Ted Rowse's *U. S. Consumer* newsletter, some New Jersey women discovered that even though *Tang* may be tasteless, it's tops for removing those brown spots that accumulate inside dishwashers. On the other hand, there is no compensation for housewives who learn that the lifetime of a General Electric lightbulb hardly measures up to the claims the company makes for it. If they knew, for example, that a bulb manufactured in pre-electronic age 1912 lasted 1000 hours, while a 1968 bulb flickers out after 750 hours, the temptation to switch to kerosene might be irresistible.

What is deception to one consumer may seem to be a deal for another, and for that reason, most deceptive practices are difficult to eradicate. Health and safety issues are far more clear cut in the view of many legislators. To the consumer, mislabeled meat—prime grade when it is only a medium grade—is simply something that must be tolerated along with watered orange juice and meatless hotdogs.

Most of the time, the seller doesn't cross over the thin line between truth and deception blatantly or obtrusively; the manuever is more like an unethical tiptoe. The thin gray line of deception mid-twentieth century style is graphically illustrated by a recent Federal Trade Commission action against *Sucrets*, a

Merck & Co. product. The commission questioned Merck's claim
that *Sucrets* killed germs on contact because one of the
ingredients was hexylresorcinol, which is potent enough to kill
strep and staph germs. After hearing testimony from all parties,
the F.T.C. examiner raised his red flag. *Sucrets* only made fleeting
contact with the throat and therefore didn't reach deepseated
germs. "Words and sentences," he concluded, "may be technically true and yet be framed in such a setting as to mislead or
deceive." Other observers detected a basic flaw in Merck's
defense. If hexylresorcinol was so effective, why didn't the
company recommend it to physicians in its highly-respected
medical manual, a bible in many doctors' offices?

Occasionally, of course, deception may be so clear cut that
a simple regulatory ruling or an amendment to an existing law can
plug a loophole and aid the buyer. Some of the conditions which
recent fur labeling actions sought to improve were so blatant as to
be ludicrous. The column on the left contains the deceptive
names of thousands of furs women are still wearing around the
nation.

False name	*Real name*
Alaska Sable	dyed skunk
Australian Seal	dyed rabbit
Blue Japanese Wolf	dyed goat
Black Pioret Fox	dyed dog
Russian Black Marten	dyed opossum

Exposure of deception in the American economy today is
so widespread that even the comic strips have caught up with the
times. As Presidential advisor Betty Furness noted in early 1968,
Mary Worth was busy exposing the old bait 'n switch routine and
the bogus contest, while Steve Roper was digging into the
unclaimed estate scheme in which unsuspecting innocents are sold
useless information. Even Pogo's Mr. Miggle was caught mislabel-
ing duck eggs.

Some consumers may find the bait 'n switch harmless, but
anyone who has jumped for an offer of a side of prime beef
wholesale if he buys a new freezer, only to wind up with a bag of
oxtails and bones instead, no longer laughs. Neither does the FTC

find anything amusing about New York distributors who flood
the Indian reservations of the western United States with tom
toms and tomahawks made on East 138th Street. The commission has asked the companies to tell it like it is. If headdresses and
silver bracelets weren't made by the Navajos, they should not be
represented to tourists as having been Indian-made.

In the furniture and clothing industries, similar tricks are
less common but adversely affect more people. The Federal Trade
Commission took action in 1968 against numerous manufacturers
in those fields. Each time the patterns were similar. Retailers of
men's clothes, large operators and small, apparently are unable to
control the desire to represent suits as either "brand new," or
"current season styling," when a good percentage of the
inventory is 15 years old. Furniture dealers, too, attract customers with the allure of private, exclusive deals. Such firms
don't normally sell to the public, they say, but "we'll make an
exception this time." In reality, a network of dummy corporations lurk in the background, charging higher prices to the customer than he'd pay in a fashionable Fifth Avenue store.

Whether it is on Indian reservations, in the flossy suburban
shopping centers surrounding New York City or in the funny-
papers, consumers are discovering that despite their affluence, the
marketplace needs to be cleansed and purged of deceptive
practices. "New business rackets are being developed and old ones
pursued and resurrected every passing day," Paul Rand Dixon
warned not long ago. "As long as suckers are born who can be
fleeced quickly and certainly with a relatively small outlay of
capital and effort, there will be found among America's entrepre-
neurs quite enough rascals to accommodate them."

Massive legislative outbursts may be needed as purgatives in
the extreme cases such as auto safety and impure meat. However,
more diligent quality control by industry is often a better answer.
Such diligence would certainly have saved the nation's largest oil
companies from the embarrassment of a survey conducted by the
North Dakota State Laboratories at Bismarck. Inspectors randomly sampled lots of gasoline. Not only did they find that
brands varied slightly in octane potency but that 105 lots among
2700 samples tested were substandard, in some cases, very
substandard. Were shady fly-by-nights the culprits? American

Oil's premium had the most failures with 13, followed by Humble and Texaco with 11 and Mobil, nine.

A little candor from the oil companies, a concession that they, too, make mistakes, would put the consumer on a more equitable plane. The same advice is valid for those radio manufacturers the government investigates periodically who claim their sets contain 12 transistors when six of them are plastic dummies. And for the producers of the facial sauna kit now being sold across the U.S. in many of the best stores. At first glance, the gadget seems a perfect gift for the wrinkle-conscious housewife. It might have been peddled that way forever had the Food and Drug Administration not detected a rather serious flaw. The water vapor rising from the sauna is not steam. What's more, the consumer could probably get more relief for her wrinkles by massaging herself with a hot towel, Federal investigators determined, or running hot water in a basin.

Free competition is the alpha and the omega of America's cherished free enterprise system, while the right of the consumer to make a choice is the philosophical fuel that powers the system. But the question that remains largely unanswered is this: who decides what the consumer will have to choose from? The quality control engineers or the marketers?

As the Florida Division of Trade Standards discovered in a survey of Miami supermarkets, sometimes there is too much choice, most of it deceptively packaged. Inspectors located ten different sizes of king-size bread that weighed between 18 and 24 ounces. The variance between regular loaves was 13 to 17 ounces.

There is no question that such deception is a burden to the budget-conscious family. The bread companies are guilty of even shadier tricks, too. According to a study made recently by the Department of Labor's Bureau of Labor Statistics, bakers in one large city recently changed the weight of the loaf from 16 ounces to 14 rather than increase prices. Diet bread, too, is not always what it seems. Federal inspectors have found that diet bread is often nothing more than regular bread, sliced thinner.

A dozen different pockets of deception could be picked for scrutiny, but the consumerists single out three as among the most worrisome—door-to-door sales, the moving industry and the lumber industry.

The door-to-door salesman has been part of the American scene since colonial days. The products he has sold over the years run the gamut from aluminum siding to zircons. Despite the rise of the large corporation the direct selling industry has blossomed into a multi-billion-dollar business. Approximately 15,000 companies operate in the field, employing 2 million salesmen. No consumerist will go to the extreme of castigating the entire industry for the $1 billion worth of frauds every year, but they will talk endlessly about the many serious problems wracking the industry. As FTC Chairman Dixon has testified in his support of a bill that would protect the buyer, the reasons for this unsavory situation are not complex. "To make a fast buck, mobility and anonymity are required. The contact with the consumer must be of short duration. It is essential that it be accompanied by confusing sales talk, vague promises and, above all, a quick and legally binding decision on the part of the victim." Their targets: the poor, the uneducated, the unsophisticated, the elderly.

FTC files show that the most common frauds involve freezers, vacuum cleaners, sewing machines, correspondence courses, intercom systems, fire alarms, aluminum siding and encyclopedias.

The sidewalk shysters employ three basic methods of fleecing the housewife. The first is the "door opener." Before the salesman can begin piling up quick and dirty dollars, he must develop sales leads. That's easy. All he does is to plant a series of advertisements in local papers, offering products at stunningly low prices complete with such come-ons as "free home demonstration," "limited time only" and "special sales price." Most of the time the ads list only a phone number; the smart con man never leaves an address. When the consumer calls the number the company representative hooks him into a free demonstration. The companies almost always have "Guild," "Institute," "American," or "United States" somewhere in the name, which is designed to reassure the buyer. What usually follows afterwards is a dreary tale of large down payments, defective products and disappearing salesmen.

Another introductory technique is the phony contest, often operated at shopping centers and theatres, according to FTC Chairman Dixon. Everybody who fills out a card wins a second prize in the contest, usually $50 toward purchase of

thousands of dollars of merchandise. In reality, there is no prize.
All the consumer wins is a visit from a high-pressure salesman
who hoodwinks him into signing an elaborate contract for some
overpriced merchandise.

A third ruse is the blind telephone call from a downtown
"boiler room." The housewife is told that the caller is taking a
survey or conducting a contest. One of these operators made the
mistake of trying to pull the wool over an FTC attorney's eyes in
1968. He was told by the mysterious caller that he would get a
valuable prize if he could supply the correct answer to the
following question:

"Who shot Abraham Lincoln?"

"Benedict Arnold."

"That's close enough, you win."

Though suburbanites are sometimes prey for shady operators, the real victims are the Americans who live in the ghettoes
from coast to coast. According to William O'Brien, an official of
HEW, salesmen weasel their way into ghetto homes by befriend-
ing the family, pretending to have a personal relationship with the
family, dining with them and even giving advice on family
problems. Each visit seems more like a social call than a sell.
Salesmen reinforce this feeling by allowing family payments to
slip a month or two. In the end, what the salesman gets out of the
time he has spent is an installment contract worth five or six
times what the family would pay if they bought the merchandise
in a store.

No one knows for certain how deep are the roots of abuse
in the direct-selling field. Professor David Caplovitz of Columbia
University, for one, believes they run deep in the ghettoes, if not
in suburbia, too. He surveyed 500 families in the New York area
and found that half had made one purchase from a door-to-door
salesman and more than a third had made subsequent purchases.

"One of the social and economic conditions in low income
areas as seen by the riot report is clearly economic exploitation of
residents," said Senator Warren Magnuson during the 1968
hearings.

Public housing projects are considered rich hunting grounds
by unscrupulous salesmen. Pretending to be employees of the
housing authority, salesmen install cabinets or appliances and
then ask the resident to sign a receipt. In a flash he is gone,

leaving the resident with a three-year installment contract. Other residents have been assaulted by salesmen disguised as employees of the school system. They inform their victims that the school requires each student to have an encyclopedia. David Caplovitz testified that he had met "Puerto Rican parents who cannot read English, who, nonetheless, agreed to purchase on credit $400 sets of encyclopedias, simply because they believed the salesman's story that their child would otherwise be forced to drop out of school."

The FTC has been escalating its attack against the sellers, issuing cease and desist orders more frequently now than ever before. Stronger action is needed, the commission believes, such as legislation modeled along the lines of British law. For years buyers have been granted a 72-hour cooling off period to consider in greater detail, in the absence of impulsive salesmen, whether they should sign the final papers.

If the United States had such a law Mrs. Victoria Scates of Washington, D. C. would have had a far different experience than she did at the hands of a slick salesman who came to her door selling stereo sets. During his pitch, Mrs. Scates mentioned that her TV set was broken. "He talked for a long time and made it sound as if it was easy to own one. He showed me how we could afford to pay for it on his easy payment plan. As a result of his persuasion, my husband picked out a TV from the salesman's pictures. We signed an agreement. The salesman told us the TV would cost $199 and would be a certain brand name. A TV was delivered the next day, but it was not like the one my husband had picked out from the pictures. It was not even the same brand name. He told me he didn't have any more of the kind we ordered." Some time later the Scates received a coupon book. The bill: $300.

In some jurisdictions, legal remedies exist to provide assistance to consumers. But most of the time, the buyer is unaware of their existence. "However, even when possessed with such knowledge," White House consumer aide Leslie Dix has declared, "the time and the expense of litigation, and the uncertainty of securing adequate relief will deter him from bringing action. . . Present enforcement has generally been ineffective in providing relief for the buyer. It is difficult to prove deception."

There are several reasons for this. Firms will sometimes repudiate the verbal commitments their salesmen have made while others, in financing sales contracts, discount the paper to a third party. This makes it nearly impossible for the consumer to get relief because he has no counterattack against the holder in due course doctrine.

Nearly half a dozen states have moved to slap restrictions on door-to-door sales, including California, Connecticut and Michigan. Many more will act soon. What is impeding the process government officials believe, is the kneejerk reaction of even such reputable firms as Fuller and Avon. Their opposition to cooling off periods is strong.

While the direct sales business grapples with reform, household movers, another established industry, have just begun to move into consumerism's range. Forty million Americans move every year, a total of 12 million households, and there are problems enough on both sides to go around. The Interstate Commerce Commission possesses regulatory power over interstate shipments which number only two million of the total but that power is limited, mostly because the movers have launched court suits in the past to keep it limited.

Yet the times are changing. The I.C.C. has been blitzed in recent months by heavy pressure from legislators and outraged consumers. These critics charge that the commission deals too gently with what they believe to be a host of deceptive and unfair practices. The complaints piling up in Washington from aroused consumers dwell on several practices in particular. They are: deliberate cost underestimates to win corporate or military bids, a ruse known as low-balling, and sloppy delivery records. The balance relate to loss and damage claims which some companies refuse to honor.

Understandably, the industry is as outraged at the critics as consumers seem to be at it. Stung by press accounts of looming congressional investigations, company spokesmen have tried to brush the reports aside by claiming that I.C.C. regulation is strong enough, or that self-regulation adequately deals with the problems without further government interference.

Where does the truth lie? *Consumer Reports*, after an exhaustive survey, concluded that 25 per cent of the consumers polled found serious fault with moving companies. The balance, however, gave unequivocally high marks to such companies as North American Van Lines, the Bekins group and Allied Van

Lines and others which had recently moved them. "Good" or
"very good" was the assessment of the majority.

What nags the consumerists is that such a large percentage should have found serious fault. That may be attribut-
able in part to the implications of a U.S. Census study showing
that of all Americans age 25 to 34 who have been to college,
36 per cent move every year. These are people whose expectations are rising, junior executives and military career men,
and they are demanding better service than the moving industry is
now providing. One would suppose that movers would go far out
of their way to please this ever-growing group of upwardly mobile
families. Repeat business from them is vital if revenues are to
keep rising. However, if preliminary congressional probes are a
valid guide, that supposition isn't as firm as it might be. "Unfair
and deceptive practices abound," a veteran Senate aide reports.
"The Interstate Commerce Commission is little more than a
handmaiden to the industry."

The moving industry has grown tremendously since World
War II but not enough, critics charge, to keep up with the
accelerating rate of family formations. Most of the large
companies are in fact sprawling networks of small, independent
truckers who lease drivers and trucks to the giants. And therein
lies some of the trouble. After a disastrous move, the customer
runs headlong into a blizzard of buckpassing and rarely gets any
satisfaction. Naturally, the majority of the industry avoids shady
tricks, at least the bulk of them don't set out to defraud
customers but the lines of command are like spaghetti and a
surprising number of people get—or think they get—cheated. If
the move occurs within a "commercial zone," an area designated
by some communities, under trucking industry pressure, where
I.C.C. jurisdiction is not allowed, the customer has nowhere to
turn but the small claims court in case of damage.

If the I.C.C. has been gentle with the industry, the
Department of Defense under Robert McNamara was frequently
aggressive with unreliable truckers. The department still keeps
tabs on the records of every trucker, since it spends nearly $1
billion a year moving servicemen and occasionally suspends and
blacklists companies after investigations have turned up evidence
contrary to the image the moving industry likes to have of itself.

The I.C.C., to be sure, is showing signs of rejuvenation under the hot spotlight of consumerism. Responding under the weight of a record number of complaints, it issued some new rules late in 1967.

Under the rules, which many consumers may still be unaware of, moving companies must:

item: notify the customer if delivery will be a day or more late.

item: acknowledge damage or loss claims within 30 days and pay or respond within four months.

item: give at least 24 hours notice when charges are going to be 10 per cent or $25 more than the original estimate, whichever is greater.

item: reweigh the load if the customer doubts the weight. (The I.C.C. discovered after sampling nearly 4000 consumers, that average weight over original estimates was 584 pounds.)

item: bear liability for the declared value of the shipment if the customer requests it and pay 50 cents per $100 of estimated value which must equal $1.25 a pound shipped. Thus, a 4000 pound load must be valued at $5000 and the charge, $25.

The question of damages and claims is an especially thorny one since the I.C.C. lacks the authority to intervene in such disputes. But generally the rules have had an impact, if nothing more than to prompt more complaints to the I.C.C. "Consumers have found they have a voice now and they are using it," commented an I.C.C. official.

A bill still under consideration by the Senate Commerce Committee would establish new machinery for settling small claims, not unlike a small claims court. But even if such a law goes on the books, consumerists believe that the moving industry must stop worrying about its image and begin to respond the rising expectations of its customers. And what customers want, according to their complaints, is more information about how to move. If there is no response from the industry, a confrontation is inevitable. One indicator of the relations between the American Movers Conference, which is the national trade association based in Washington, and the I.C.C. Callers are referred by I.C.C. officials to the trade association for information about the industry.

With sales exceeding $2 billion a year, the softwood lumber industry is a vital ingredient of the American economy. Its products are in millions of homes and office buildings while company payrolls provide livelihoods for millions of workers. But the industry is rapidly becoming almost as controversial as it is prosperous. According to Congressman John Dingell, and numerous government regulators, dishonesty is so widespread that an honest retailer must imitate dishonest competitors if he wants to remain in business very long.

Dingell's charge has been reinforced by a little-publicized study of the industry by the Federal Trade Commission. The report said, in part, that "the masquerading of low grade lumber for high grade lumber has bilked consumers of millions of dollars; has lowered the margin of structural safety in innumerable dwellings; and, in the affected market areas, has impaired competitive moves among surviving wholesalers, retailers, and contractors."

For the consumer, the message is clear—and shocking. The buyer often pays premium prices for lumber that has no relation to the grade stamped on it. At the same time, finished sizes are shrinking rapidly. Fifty years ago, for example, 13/16 inch was a common thickness for dressed 1-inch boards. By 1929, 25/32 inch had become more common; the 3/4 inch board appeared in 1956 and the industry is now proposing to seek a 5/8 inch board.

Moreover, Washington consumerists complain, there is the appearance of regulatory standards where virtually none exist. Congressman Dingell, for one, charges that the whole system of grading lumber is dishonest and unrealistic because it is not based on the actual strength of each board. "There is a false representation made on every board graded," Dingell claims. For example, West Coast Douglas fir is nearly 50 per cent stronger than it is in the Rocky Mountain area yet the Forest Products Laboratory of the U.S. Department of Agriculture grades them identically. He also argues that even though some grades of Southern yellow pine vary in strength by as much as 500 pounds per square inch, all are assigned the highest value without protest.

At least part of the problem lies with the regulations themselves about which most consumers are ignorant. Graded lumber is defined as lumber which is sorted as to size, prospective use and quality. At least 80 per cent of softwood lumber that is consumed domestically is graded accordingly. Grade-marked lumber, on the other hand, bears a permanent stamp designating strength and sometimes size. According to the FTC study, federal, state and local building codes require lumber to be grade-marked and then limit and qualify the use of the lower grades of common yard lumber. "This encourages some buyers," the FTC concluded, "to purchase unmarked, low grade yard lumber and 'upgrade it,' either by affixing to it a mark designating a higher grade, or by mixing it with grade-marked, higher-grade lumber."

Some of the misgrading occurs at the mill and some in the yards, the FTC discovered. For that reason, building inspectors have been hard put to assign the blame once lumber flows out into the distribution system. The extent to which purchasing in order to upgrade, the FTC further determined, can be judged by looking at prices. Prices for higher grades have been moving up in the face of a general drop in the demand for lumber when legitimate grade-marking of the lower grades of lumber has been increased.

The FTC found, moreover, that "low grade lumber is difficult to sell when marked; when unmarked, it commands a premium." Upgraded lumber has accounted for a substantial share of the industry's sales in the District of Columbia, California, New York and Texas. For all that, deceptive practices aren't confined solely to upgrading, other government reports show. Some misgrading may be due to dyeing of the wood even before the grading process. Congressman John Dingell has suggested that the use of cherry brown dye makes inferior lumber look like Douglas fir and also serves to cover up fungus and other defects.

In theory, the policeman of the industry is the American Lumber Standards Committee composed of 23 members who are named by the Secretary of Commerce. Although the group has evidence of many wrongs, Dingell charges, it has never used its power to decertify any of the companies who allegedly are guilty of misgrading lumber. Furthermore, the Committee budgeted only $59,000 last year to oversee the grading of 20 billion board feet of lumber worth more than $1 billion.

For many years in America, deception has been tolerated as the natural order of things, the price of progress and the descendent of good, old Boston Yankee know-how. Whenever strong protests have billowed up in Washington in the past some regulatory agency or another, when it could no longer avoid taking action, issued a trade regulation law. "Any survey of the old trade regulation laws," Betty Furness has said, "quickly reveals that consumer protection in most cases was not the real objective. Most of these laws were intended to protect the vested interests...when I look over the laws passed in the name of 'consumer protection' in the United States since 1900, I wonder if we have made much progress over the years." But new laws are not the measure—at least not the only measure—of the rise of consumer protection sentiment in Washington.

The Federal Trade Commission, for example, has set out to root out deception by clarifying the requirements of existing law and to encourage voluntary compliance with the laws. With a budget of only $14 million a year, which is equal to what General Motors earns in one morning, the commission reached the conclusion last year that it was patently impossible to police the nation's $800 billion economy by bringing a handful of adversary actions against lawbreakers. "To have attempted it," Chairman Dixon recently told Congress, "would have been a futile as for police to depend solely on sirens and the passing out of tickets to achieve safety on the highways." Instead, Dixon reasoned, "common sense dictated that if trade laws were to be obeyed, only the willingness (and self interest) of reputable businessmen to comply with them would achieve a fair and orderly market-place."

During the last fiscal year, FTC conducted 1200 investigations of deceptive practices, from gas station promotional games to misleading tire guarantees and franchise bilking schemes to fraudulent auto transmission repair shops.

Corrective action was also taken against false claims for the effectiveness of products offered to relieve and treat hemorrhoids and toward developing scientific evidence designed to tone down exaggerated claims for *Anacin* and *Bufferin.* Studies have also been undertaken to learn whether the automakers are honoring warranties.

Once known as a political dumping ground for Congressmen's pals, the FTC has emerged fighting and now battles harder for consumer protection than any other agency except the S.E.C.

There is broad recognition within the agency that headline-grabbing legal actions against corporations are counter-productive. Whatever the merits of the case, it lands in the courts and remains there for years while the deceptions continue apace. The guidance and voluntary approach has already produced better results. Three hundred and sixty rule and guide compliance matters were disposed of in fiscal 1967, on the basis of assurances that the practices had been discontinued.

A sample rulemaking effort which may aid consumers more than if messy lawsuits had been attempted, involved the glass fiber curtain, drapery and fabric industry. The industry had failed in the past to disclose that skin irritation could result from the washing and handling of such products. The industry, which consists of 1,100 manufacturers who produce 6 million sets of curtains a year and 15 million pairs of draperies valued at $60 million, attended a public hearing at FTC headquarters and a trade regulation resulted. Consumers are now warned.

Though deception still exists, the effort in this decade to annihilate it is unmatched in the Nation's history. "*Caveat emptor* is dead and buried," Chairman Dixon declares, "let the seller beware is the new climate."

Doubt

chapter 9

"I'm a consumer and I hate it," a young man told Presidential adviser Betty Furness at a meeting early in 1968. "It's the most frustrating thing I do."

The young man's problem is shared by us all. When he makes an effort to make a sensible, meaningful choice among the thousands of products in the marketplace, he is often unable to accomplish his aim.

When he and his wife buy a washing machine, does he know how well it performs, or how long it will last? The answer is no, because the information, which is known to the manufacturer, is not provided to the consumer.

When a housewife buys a roll of paper towels, can she choose the best buy among the 33 different sizes of packages that confront her? The answer is again no, unless the housewife stops to compute cost per sheet for every one of the different packages.

When a young lady buys a facial cream, does she know what is in it? The answer is no, because the ingredients are seldom listed underneath the promises.

In short, the American consumer is in a perpetual state of bewilderment and doubt because no matter how he may try, he often doesn't know what he is buying. He doesn't know because he isn't told.

To many consumer advocates, the doubt that plagues the American buyer is the central issue, the fundamental failing of the system. It is not protection the buyer needs, say the consumerists. It is information. If he knows what a product does, how much it costs per ounce, how long it will last, how safe it is,

what the warranty behind it means, then he doesn't need the
protection of the state or Federal government. He can make a
valid choice according to his needs and resources without having
to run for help. The argument that the consumer makes the final
choice and is the final arbiter of success or failure of a product is
no more than a convenient fiction. The fact is that every legal
means is used to deprive the consumer of that power. In a highly
complex economy, with massive investments of time and money
tied up in their wares, any marketer who simply told the
consumer about his product and then let it fend for itself would
be considered a fool by his fellow marketers. The seller plans
ahead, and assures his market as best he can before he places a
new product on its shelves or in its showrooms. The purpose of
the product is to sell, and sales cannot be guaranteed if the
consumer is operating on his own. He is conditioned, like one of
Pavlov's dogs, by annual advertising expenditures of $17 billion.

In *The New Industrial State*, J.K. Galbraith expounded
on this marketplace reality in blunt terms: "The general effect of
sales effort, defined in the broadest terms, is to shift the locus of
decision in the purchase of goods from the consumer where it is
beyond control to the firm where it is subject to control. . . The
specific strategy, though it varies somewhat between industries
and over time, consists first in recruiting a loyal or automatic
corps of customers. This is variously known as building customer
loyalty or brand recognition. To the extent that it is successful, it
means that the firm has a stable body of custom which is secure
against mass defection which might follow from freely exercised
consumer choice."

That is a good definition of a planned economy, but not
the bugaboo of a state-planned one. The U.S. economy is to a
considerable extent an industry-planned economy. The plans
don't work perfectly, or all the time. But they usually do. The
occasional flops are employed to suggest the reality of consumer
control, with the *Edsel* the favorite example. But the flop of the
Edsel serves only to reinforce the point; it was a rare and unusual
sight to see a giant of American industry fail at marketing
a car that nobody wanted anyway. Such ventures usually succeed.

Although it seems eminently fair and democratic that the
consumer be told more about the products he is considering
buying, the prospect of a nation of intelligent consumers seems to

horrify many on the other side of the store counter. With 200 million consumers of widely varying means and motivations, however, it would seem that any product with any merit at all could find buyers. Progressively fewer economists and Congressmen, and even businessmen, can find any reason why the consumer should not be given more information to aid him in his choice. And many reasons can be found to show why he should be better informed. An unwise and uninformed purchase can fail to satisfy a customer's needs and wants, thereby wasting his money and costing the company a future customer. The frustration of being misled by a clever but uninformative advertisement may also annoy the consumer greatly. It is probably safe to say that every adult buyer carries in his mind a list of prejudices against products and entire companies which are the result of bad experiences. (No doubt many of the prejudices are as irrelevant as the advertisements that led him astray in the first place.)

The consumer of today is wiser, better educated, and better warned by the battles of the 1960s. His blacklist of products is becoming a more reasoned one, his sales resistance is climbing steadily, his demands to know what he is buying steadily more strident. More often now, he knows what he doesn't know about the marketplace. He is aware of his doubts, conscious of his ignorance, and suspicious that his ignorance is deliberately nurtured.

There are two main areas of confusion that confront the consumer: packaging and labeling, and the function, performance, and reliability of goods and services. The products that raise these doubts in him can range from a box of macaroni to automobile insurance.

Prices, Packages, and Labels

The problem of packaging and pricing is best revealed by having a reputable businessman explain industry's approach. At a symposium considering "Freedom of Information in the Marketplace" at the University of Missouri held in December, 1966, Lloyd E. Skinner, president of a large pasta firm, explained his methods. He meant his statement to justify the state of affairs on the storeshelf, but it works out the other way. Said Skinner: "We pack macaroni in 7-ounce, 8-ounce, 16-ounce, 24-ounce and 2-

and 3-pound packages. There are reasons for this. Why do we make a seven-ounce line? Because some of our competitors do not use 100 percent durum wheat, and although it is generally agreed that durum makes the best macaroni, he sells his 8-ounce blend at 2 for 25 cents. This is a psychological price. Psychological pricing means that an item priced at 19 cents will move better than a similar item priced at 20 cents. Manufacturers who are using 100 per cent durum wheat may want to get the 2-for-25-cent shelf price, the same as that of the fellow who is using a poorer quality of raw material. The quality manufacturer is in a squeeze; he is not trying to hurt anybody but is trying to get his product out where it will move, and he moves this merchandise by selling a 7-ounce of 100 per cent durum instead of an 8-ounce blend. Psychological pricing has become very important in stores."

A double dose of confusion is thus bestowed on the purchasers of Mr. Skinner's macaroni. The superior quality of his product is very carefully hidden—its higher cost per ounce is hidden from any consumer who does not search out the net weight. Consumers who operate on the assumption that better goods cost more, which is usually the case and is the case here, will be confounded. Those who have run up against the prepayday pinch, which is traditionally macaroni and cheese time, and want the most volume for their money, must conduct an on-the-spot analysis of the package's printed matter to find the more economical buy. Mr. Skinner's opponent in this battle of the macroni contributes to the confusion by cleverly concealing the fact that his macaroni is a better buy in terms of bulk.

A great amount of storeshelf competition follows this topsy-turvy pattern of concealing the means of making objective value comparisons. A package of *Plumrose* sliced ham, which is a superior product, is priced close to the lower-grade brands. Ounce for ounce, this is plainly impossible; *Plumrose* is sold in 4-1/2 ounce packages, while the cheaper brands are usually sold in eight-ounce packages. If the consumer happens to notice the difference, all is well. But if he doesn't—if he just grabs at the *Plumrose* because he knows it is good and the price seems right, then the game isn't discovered until there isn't enough ham for lunch.

Simply put, "psychological pricing" is a device to hide price-quality relationships among products from the buyer, to

remove them from his decision-making processes. The situation
becomes chaotic on the drug shelf. At one point, the number of
different sizes of toothpastes reached a high mark of 57. Weights
were broken down to tenths of an ounce. Prices among tubes
with different weights were often the same, and some larger tubes
were cheaper than the slightly smaller ones. To determine
whether *Crest* or *Fact*, two fluoridated toothpastes of similar
virtue in preventing decay (according to the American Dental
Association endorsement they both bear proudly on their
backsides), it is necessary to compute 3.25 ounces at 51 cents
versus 4.6 ounces at 61 cents.

The hope, obviously, is that the consumer won't bother,
but will reach for the tube that is more familiar to him.
Familiarity is primarily a function of the number of times the
product name is repeated in ads, surely the greatest irrelevancy of
all. Said Richard Barber, former counsel for the Senate Judiciary
Committee's antitrust and monopoly subcommittee, at the same
meeting where Mr. Skinner spoke: "Discernable is the aim of the
sellers of consumer goods to minimize price competition and
place a principal reliance on advertising, packaging and assorted
nonprice tactics as a means of sale. The form of these tactics may
vary, but their basic character remains essentially the same, for
seller behavior is typically aimed less at informing the prospective
buyer than at frustrating objective value comparisons."

The logic is simple enough, and one can see easily enough
why businessmen latched on to it so readily. To compete on
terms of price often seems to threaten price wars, and thus
lowered profits. Lowered profits are not considered good
business. Many consumers also prefer or are obliged to pay a little
less for a somewhat lower quality product, so it is possible to
compete on terms of the price-quality relationship. This method,
too, is often shunned; it is considered suicidal to speak of one's
product in anything less than superlatives. All products are "the
best." In the end, the safest course is often to sell on the basis of
irrelevancies; there need be no deception at all employed to sell a
product on some basis other than its value. Colossal amounts of
research go into the names of products, their package sizes,
designs and colors.

The games manufacturers play with their packages and
labels and pricetags was the object of a legislative battle waged

over the space of five years—the fight for the Fair Packaging and Labeling Act. The act, which is more familiarly known as the truth-in-packaging act, finally passed in 1966, and in the words of *Consumer Reports*, it was "something of a legislative miracle." The miracle is not the ingredients to the bill, but that anything passed at all against the opposition of a $100-billion industry. Michigan Senator Philip Hart, who sponsored the bill and fought it through to its ambiguous conclusion said of it: "If history, as Francis Bacon claims, does indeed 'make a man wise,' then a wise man would not even advocate such a bill, no matter how persuasive the evidence."

The basic goal of the bill was best characterized by Marya Mannes writing in the *New York Times*. "Most of us," she lamented, "are simply too busy or too tired or too harassed to take a computer, a slide rule, and an M.I.T. graduate to market and figure out what we're buying."

Senator Hart's objective was to require the imposition of standards on the size and weight of packages so that consumers would have an easier time in their comparison shopping. No attempt was made to reduce the number of brands in the marketplace, but simply to reduce the number of packages. Other objects of the bill included banishing such phrases as the "jumbo quart" or "giant half gallon," and systematizing phrases such as "family size" or "large economy size," which mean different things to different manufacturers and therefore mean nothing to the consumer.

The law as it passed did achieve some major advances. It required the Food and Drug Administration and the Federal Trade Commission to set standards for disclosing net quantity on a package, and all packages now show their weight in reasonably large type on the main display panel. The law also requires that ingredients be listed in order of their proportion. If a pancake syrup, for example, is listed as containing corn syrup, cane sugar syrup, and maple sugar syrup, the major ingredient is then corn syrup, or as Dr. Harvey Wiley would have preferred it back at the turn of the century, glucose. There is no deception at work unless a glucose-based syrup is priced as though it came out of a tree in Vermont.

The rest of the truth-in-packaging act suffers from a defect that many consider fatal. The government was deprived of the power to establish standard package sizes as a device to reduce package proliferation and the resulting confusion. Instead, standardization was made voluntary, with the Departments of Commerce and Health, Education, and Welfare empowered to make only suggestions, and to seek legislation if the voluntary approach failed. This provision was a major victory for the bill's opponents. There is nothing quite so futile as a law which permits the government to ask for more laws to accomplish the purposes of the first law. This is one reason why Ralph Nader wryly calls the packaging act the "most deceptive package of all."

However, the voluntary approach has brought some results which can only help simplify life for the supermarket shopper. By mid-1968, industries had agreed to make the following reduction in numbers of different size packages:

Cereals—from 33 to 16 sizes.

Detergents—24 to 6.

Toothpaste—57 to 5.

Paper towels—33 to 8.

Dry milk—20 to 10.

Jams and jellies—16 to 10.

Green olives—50 to 15.

Coffee—10 to 8.

The Macaroni Manufacturers Association has, incidentally, formed a study committee. The potato chip industry was among the holdouts. It still offers the consumer 71 different sizes of packages. In the main, however, the device of leaving the execution of a law's toothless suggestion up to an administrative agency has had the result predicted by dissatisfied customers ranging from Senator Warren Magnuson on down (he suggested that the bill shouldn't even be called a packaging act, but simply a labeling act). The pace has been slow and uncertain to the point where White House aides and congressmen alike were predicting that the battle would have to be fought all over again.

Product Performance

One of the more useless questions a consumer can ask is: How good is it? Another question—how long will it last?—is seldom answered. The salesman doesn't know, and the manufacturer usually won't tell. In all the nation, there is only one private source of information on the reliability of products such as automobiles and automatic washers—*Consumer Reports'* frequency-of-repair records. These are based on reader polls, and the simple statistical compilations are revealing. *Norge* and *Westinghouse* washers, for example, have had repair records below average for eight long years. *Norge* machines were until recently manufactured by Borg-Warner, hardly a fly-by-night concern. The unblemished record of bad performance cannot therefore be an unlucky accident anymore than *Maytag*'s record of superior performance over the years is a lucky accident. Any large manufacturer can tell how long his appliance will last, what part will likely age first, and how much repairs will cost in each succeeding year, and when the crossover point between repairing or replacing is reached.

Only Borg-Warner and Westinghouse know the reasons behind the dismal record of their washers. But the machines have obviously continued to sell on the market, and the matter of how good they were obviously was distinctly secondary to the sales picture. The record makes a fiction of the standard industry claim that it depends on brand loyalty for success. The truth is that the U.S. market is so large that new and unsuspecting customers are plentiful.

Complaints on product performance are so numerous that consumer affairs adviser Betty Furness felt compelled to make this suggestion to the American Marketing Association in December of 1967: "I think the consumer should be told by his marketer what's actually in the box he buys. It may be revolutionary to suggest that the manufacturer or the marketer give the consumer the basic facts about the design life of a product. But I believe it's his due. Why shouldn't the housewife know that there are 'X' number of hours of service in her washing machine or that the life expectancy of a toaster falls short of a golden wedding anniversary?... The manufacturer knows, and the marketer knows, what the design life of their product is. Shouldn't the consumer also know?"

There is no question that the suggestion is revolutionary, at least in the public marketplace. The government wouldn't think of buying a piece of electronic equipment for an aircraft or spacecraft without knowing its reliability and lifetime. For that matter, a manufacturer selling in the open market wouldn't buy from a subcontractor or a supplier without knowing all he possibly could about the items he is purchasing. This is eminent good business sense. But to extend the right to know to the consumer is so alien to the American way of business that Federal legislation will probably be required, if only to police the requirement, if not to get it done in the first place. Compulsory or voluntary standards to define performance and reliability would be necessary to prevent some manufacturers from playing fast and loose with their claims.

The idea is reasonable nonetheless, and the logic behind such a requirement is inescapable. The consumer has a right to know, and the effects would not be at all devastating to the manufacturer. Given equal technology, manufacturers competing for a share of the market with a certain appliance make certain basic tradeoffs between price and quality. They may choose to aim for that part of the market that demands high quality regardless of price, or that part which is willing to take less in exchange for saving some money. Declarations of performance level and design lifetime would not, as many industry voices have claimed, reduce the number of products on the market to one each. It is true that a product whose quality doesn't measure up to its price would suffer in sales unless added attention were to be paid to the engineering or preparation of the product. And indeed it would be, resulting in a general upgrading of the quality of industry's wares all across the board.

If the consumer movement is able to maintain any momentum, serious consideration of product performance and reliability seems inevitable. The trial balloon launched by Miss Furness was no more than a gentle warning. It was not on President Johnson's shopping list of 1968 consumer legislation. But the President's Commission on Product Safety is already addressing itself to the issue of hazardous performance, and Congressional committees are already collecting evidence on other aspects of the problem.

In the drug industry, it has already happened. Drugs are no longer able to avoid the elementary requirement that they do what their advertisements claim, and that they be able to do at least something for the consumer who pays for them. One far-reaching section of the 1962 drug act requires that all drugs, new and old, must be proven effective before they are sold. The bioflavinoids, a heavily-advertised hero of the cold war of a few years ago which do absolutely nothing for cold sufferers, are marked for extinction. Throat lozenges with a dash of antibiotics in them—equally useless—are likely to follow. The end result, if the task is ever completed, will be to remove one large—and expensive—questionmark from the consumer's mind as he seeks relief from a minor complaint. Since the patent-medicine industry is a multi-million dollar business, savings to the consumer from removal of worthless nostrums will be enormous. As a bonus, he is more likely to avoid the obvious danger of trying to treat an incipient strep throat with orange-flavored candy. Medical doctors, equally mesmerized by detail men from the drug companies, will also be helped by stricter controls on the efficacy of prescription drugs.

Short of the ultimate revelation of a product's worth, much can be accomplished in the form of fuller disclosure. To cite just one example, automobiles, which are the most expensive purchase a consumer makes next to his house, reveal practically nothing about their performance except horsepower. But the Federal Highway Administration is working on criteria which will make it possible to measure other performance indices. Tires will be among the first to be graded. Braking ability of various model cars will be revealed to customers. And, perhaps most revealing and important, the rate of accident involvement of all car makes and models will eventually be published by the government as a guide to the consumer's choice—and to the manufacturer's engineers.

The list of products which could use fuller disclosure is virtually infinite, and the results would often be quite startling. One of the nation's most heavily advertised products, for example, is gasoline. A mid-1968 study done by the government disclosed that gasolines are almost identical in their prime characteristic, octane rating. Of 14 regular-grade brands sold in the Northeast, tests showed the octane rating varied from a low of 94.6 to a high of 96.5. Premium grades ranged from 99.7 to 101.1. Ample evidence that gasoline companies often swap gas when they suffer distribution problems shows well enough that the major difference between brands is whether the companies have drafted a tiger or a flying horse to push them. Additives pay a very small role, if any. One top-rated gasoline, *Amoco*, contains no additives at all.

Warranties

One apparently helpful step has been taken by those industries that are willing to underwrite the reliability of their products. This is the warranty. A warranty does not guarantee that the product will operate as advertised, but it at least promises that the machine will be repaired at little or no charge if it fails to operate at all.

But warranties, legions of consumers have found, are not always what they seem. The problem has many faces. Some warranties are designed with the deliberate intention of leaving the consumer guessing. One technique is to enclose a handsomely embossed document with the word "warranty" printed in giant letters across the top—underlain by a thoroughly indigestible chunk of technical verbiage that only an engineer can decipher. Another device is the partial warranty. An *Easy* washing machine purchased in 1965, for example, bore a perfectly legible warranty, with many parts carefully listed, and an exploded diagram to show the parts covered. The list and the diagram seemed complete to the layman. But when the washer's transmission died, the company was called and asked whether the warranty covered the $75 repair charge. The answer was no. The neatly numbered, listed, and diagramed parts, a company representative rather apologetically explained, "are the parts that don't break down."

This particular machine was replaced by a *Maytag*, which bears a more thorough warranty as well as a good repair record according to the *Consumer Reports* reader polls. But the *Maytag* warranty clearly states that no other warranty, either "express or implied" can be construed to apply to the machine. This bit of wordage, very common in industry, is an attempt to free a product of the responsibility to live up to any other claims or representations made in advertisements. Even without the hyperbole of ads, any product or machine carries an implied warranty within the description of its purpose. A washer is sold for the purpose of washing clothes in a reasonably satisfactory manner. If it does a demonstrably poor job, the company is liable, and the nation's courts have ruled many times over that a product must live up to its intended purpose and do it at least adequately. Rulings have also held that the manufacturer is the one responsible, no matter how many middlemen have been engaged in passing the product along to the final buyer. Thus a company is technically obligated to replace a product that performs substantially below the average for its type.

But in practice, this seldom happens. For one thing, consumers are so inculcated with the doctrine of *caveat emptor* that they accept occasional bad luck on a new purchase as a part of the game, as though it were a lottery. Those who do rebel must make nuisances of themselves by bombarding the president of the company or its public relations staff with letters (that is what customer relations staffs are for, and many are surprisingly responsive to legitimate squawks). The other alternative is to sue. A suit complaining of an exploding bottle of *Coca-Cola* was successfully prosecuted by lawyer Melvin Belli, and many cases against the unsafe suspensions of *Corvairs* were settled out of court in favor of the plaintiffs. But clearly, few consumers have the time, the money, the extra energy, and the nerve to take on a giant of American industry, nor are the courts geared to police the marketplace.

Thus the warranty provides a handy means of bypassing the courts. It gives an extra advantage to the seller—it limits the liability of the manufacturer to the express conditions of the warranty, or at least attempts to. Thus it is critically important in large purchases to determine beforehand what exclusions there are. With a warrantied product, holding a company responsible for an excluded component can be more difficult than if there were no warranty at all.

Some warranties cover everything, some exclude labor costs and certain parts. Many take no responsibility for "normal" (an endlessly arguable word) wear and tear. Some prorate the cost of replacement of parts which wear out before their time, such as car batteries. Some, most notably automobiles, require positive and specific action on the part of the buyer to keep the warranty in force. One forgotten oil change, and the entire warranty can be voided.

There are so many vagaries and variations in the warranty business that both the legislative and executive branches of government are struggling to find ways of bringing order to the system. But writing legislation is proving to be a difficult task. The Federal Trade Commission was enlisted to write a "truth in warranties" act in 1967. A year later nothing had emerged, due to corporate pressure. The Senate Commerce Committee had meanwhile stated its intention to look into the matter, but problems of finding proper standards and means of enforcement indicated that 1969 is the earliest that hearings can be held, with legislation perhaps years away. Until the warranty business is standardized, it is wisest to have all warranties, particularly their exclusions and conditions, explained in detail, and if trouble develops to be prepared to insist that the manufacturer live up to his implied warranty even if he has clearly stated that he would rather not.

Product Servicing

A corollary problem to the warranty mess is the difficulty of finding proper product-servicing in the marketplace. This is not by any means a problem solely of industry's creation. On the contrary, it is a problem that plagues industry as much as it does the consumer. For reasons which are very difficult to establish, the repairman is no longer an attractive profession to a nation rich in the tradition of the Yankee tinkerer. One reason is that the traditional source of home repairmen, the family, has petered out. Plumbers once raised their sons to be plumbers, passing them the business when they came of age while father retired to Florida. For a variety of reasons, children are nowadays less interested in emulating their parents, particularly in the blue-collar and dirty-hand professions.

Recently, industry has begun to take steps to fill the void created by sociology. TV producers, automobile manufacturers, and appliance manufacturers run training schools for repairmen. But these companies often find that their students learn enough to take jobs with the manufacturer himself, or one of his competitors, for the better pay and higher status.

Given the best of intentions, therefore, companies still find it difficult to live up to the promises in their ads and warranties. They also find it difficult—if they try at all—to control the prices repair shops charge, and the outright frauds they perpetrate. A

high-ranking official of Sylvania Electric Products in Washington
struggles his weighty color TV into his car and drives it to the
repair shop, rather than pay the $10 house call. Repairmen still
make more house calls than doctors, but the gap is rapidly
closing.

All sides to the problem are at a loss what to do. One fairly
obvious answer is to reduce the need for repairs with better
engineering and quality control at the factory. A great portion of
repairs on new products consists in fixing mistakes made at the
factory. Since engineering and quality control has at present little
to do with the salability of a product as opposed to its
performance, the compulsion to take this step is not very strong.

The Price of Money

Consumers expect to pay for money they borrow, or for
products they buy on installment plans. Some extra charge is
expected when one receives the use of a product he has not yet
paid for. But what is the price of these privileges?

The truth-in-lending act of 1968, which will show how
much credit costs, is almost unique in the history of consumer
legislation and perhaps the most revolutionary. The bill is stronger
than the original introduced by Senator Paul Douglas of Illinois
eight years before. It was, as the gap in time indicates, a tough fight.

With a consumer installment debt exceeding $100 billion,
the need for such a law was critical. And the almost uniform
inability of any consumer to figure out the true rate of interest he
was being charged left him not only in doubt, but in total
ignorance.

Starting July 1, 1969, banking, department stores, home
mortgage lenders, finance and loan companies, and other credit
establishments must reveal their annual rate of interest. A bank
that says it lends money at 4-3/4 per cent, discounted in advance,
now must reveal that the true annual rate for such a loan is 9 per
cent. Revolving-charge accounts, shoehorned into the bill after six
months of hard labor by Missouri Representative Leonor Sullivan,
which formerly cost "1-1/2 per cent per month on the unpaid
balance" now must state that the price is 18 per cent per year.
Money-lenders such as Household Finance Corp., which offer

easy conditions but correspondingly stiff charges, will have to declare annual charges of up to 36 per cent or more.

There will still be pitfalls. Consider this example. Both Sears, Roebuck and Co. and J. C. Penney Co. charge 1-1/2 per cent per month on the unpaid balance for their revolving-credit accounts. But the cash costs at Sears can be much higher than at Penney's. Sears computes its charges before subtracting the monthly payment, Penney's after. Thus a consumer who frugally pays half of his $200 balance in the first month will be charged 1-1/2 per cent of $200 at Sears, and Sear's effective interest rate is 36 per cent in such a case. The charge at Penney's will be 1-1/2 per cent of $100. Even with the truth-in-lending bill, there is still no substitute for some careful study of the credit policies of all money-lenders. The law helps by requiring all those who do not deduct payments before computing charges to state that curious fact on the bill and contract.

Auto Insurance

The more thoughtful of this nation's consumers have recently discovered a whole new set of doubts connected with the family car. There are questions that even the most careful reading of the contract will not answer. Key among them are: Will the rates be unfairly raised? Will the policy be canceled? Will the company still exist next year? Is the cost too high?

When a Senate antitrust and monopoly subcommittee began a study of auto insurance in 1968, some of its discoveries staggered even the staffers. More than $120 billion has been collected in premiums by the industry since 1930 for liability, property damage and collision insurance. Only $60.8 has been paid back to cover claims. The massive income over outgo of the industry—$22 billion in the last five years alone—goes into investments and other enterprises, as well as overhead. The return on these other activities, conducted with the consumer's money, is seldom applied to the companies' insurance operations as a means of reducing premiums. Profits made on a consumer's payments are pocketed.

But if a consumer should have an accident, he is treated as if he has singlehandedly threatened to put the company under. Many companies raise rates when a driver is involved in an accident that is not his fault. In all but a handful of states, companies can cancel policies for any reason, or no reason at all. Most avoid or exclude certain occupations—those marked with a high proportion of Negroes (chauffeurs and actors are considered poor risks), or those over 65. Drivers under 25, who are the best drivers in terms of visual acuity and reflexes, are charged huge rates to cover their imagined irresponsibility. All told there are more risk categories than companies. The commissioner of insurance for the state of Pennsylvania, David O. Maxwell, calculated that there are a grand total of 104,000 different combinations of risks on the road today according to the definition of the insurance industry.

Each company's standards are different. A driver who qualifies for a reduced rate with one company may be socked with a surcharge by another. Many are considered so undesirable that they are thrown into an "assigned risk" pool, where each company takes pot luck and a certain number of imagined losers. In California in 1967, 245,350 drivers were tossed into this pool. All were charged higher rates than "normal" drivers. Yet 71 per cent of these risks had absolutely clean driving records.

Everyone can buy a policy if he is willing to pay the price, but it is becoming steadily more difficult to keep it. Since 1961, 80 companies have gone out of business, leaving 300,000 people with claims against them stranded. Many of these were small outfits which, unable to compete with the giants in the industry, accepted the drivers the other companies rejected, or canceled. No one even keeps an accurate count of yearly cancellations, but joining the Army or moving into crowded or ghetto areas in a city is a prime reason for being dropped. Sometimes, agents whose clients begin generating too many claims may be dropped, and all their clients—good and bad risks—are canceled.

Even at its best, with companies, clients, and claimants acting in utter honesty, the system suffers serious flaws. Court settlements range from the ridiculously high to the pathetically low. Justice, if it comes at all, can be delayed for three or four years because of jammed court calendars. When a case does finally come to trial, witnesses are gone, memories are dim, juries are bored, and justice is often not served.

"Mr. Chairman and members of the committee," Rhode Island insurance commissioner Ralph A. Petrarca told the Senate committee, "our present automobile insurance system, based as it is on the concepts of liability and negligence, is a mess."

In May of 1968, President Johnson signed a congressional resolution calling for a "comprehensive study and investigation" of the auto insurance system. The study will take two years, and cost as much as $2 million.

Such problems as these seldom represent any crime, or illegal act. They do not classify as dangerous or deceptive sins of commission. They are unethical, dishonest sins of omission. They are therefore difficult to grasp, or even to comprehend as an issue. For years, the American consumer has paid his auto insurance with no more than a brief wince, made his supermarket purchases in the firm belief that he was a wise buyer, and purchased an appliance with faith in its brand name. But as he becomes aware of his ignorance, or conversely tries to replace it with knowledge, the doubts generated by his inability to buy rationally in the marketplace have made him steadily more skeptical. It is significant to note that brand-name loyalty has been dropping in recent years, despite the steady rise in advertising. House brands are climbing rapidly in sales. One sure reason is that they are a safe bet to be more economical than the brand name. That is one of the best safe bets a consumer can make, so he makes it. Too much of everything else is guesswork.

Marketers, advertisers, and producers complain that this trend is bad for the nation—and leave it at that. The root cause of the disaffection that now exists, they suggest, is cynicism, a loss of faith caused by one too many frustrating trips to the store.

The irony is that industry could overcome this cynicism and serve its own ends by providing the consumer more information. Wisconsin Attorney General Bronson LaFollette attempted to make this point to a group of marketers at a National Association of Manufacturers meeting in 1968: "Without truth in packaging, the system rewards those who can confuse the consumer the most. Under such circumstances the traditional free enterprise system does not operate the way it is supposed to. Consumer confusion was the key to success rather than consumer satisfaction. Have we reached the point in this country where success depends upon fooling the consumer rather than pleasing him? I hope not."

La Follette's point is well taken: a product whose consumer support is based on satisfaction is in a much more sound position than one based on a handsome package and a whirlwind advertising campaign designed to control the buyer. One grows suspicious of products that are advertised incessantly, year after year. The implication is that they cannot stand on their own two feet. Any TV-watcher can add up in his own mind his amount of exposure to ads for plain aspirin, compared to those for *Anacin* or *Bufferin*—neither of which contains any analgesic other than aspirin for the relief of a headache. *Bufferin* and *Excedrin* attack each other regularly on TV—yet both are made by Bristol-Myers. *Anacin* attacks *Excedrin*, claiming it contains much more of the pain reliever that "doctors recommend most" than the "extra-strength" pill. The comparison is deceptive, since *Excedrin* employs two different pain-relievers, and therefore less aspirin than does *Anacin*. *Excedrin* counterattacks with humorous commercials about husbands making model planes in bed, and buzzing their wives into *Excedrin* headache Number 138. All attack the consumer's basic failing as a fit subject for the marketer; he still takes "aspirin" for a headache, and all manner of effort must be extended to overcome his habit of using the generic name (which, incidentally, was once Bayer's trademark until its common usage reduced it to everyday status).

That is free enterprise of a sort, but an orderly marketplace, where every product is what it seems to be, would perhaps be freer still. The costs of perpetuating doubt and confusion are huge. Bristol-Myers earned $465 million in 1966. Fully 28 per cent of that—$130 million—was spent on advertising. The company marketed twenty new products that year. Its recent batting average has been one marketing success out of three tries—it generally doesn't bother developing the new products in its labs until checking the marketing opportunities first. If this raises questions about the company's economic health, its net profits on revenues in 1966 were 8.6 per cent, or $40 million. Who pays? The consumer, the company, and its competition all pay more in a chaotic marketplace. Perhaps these inefficiencies and social costs preserve the competitive system. But perhaps not. Bristol-Myers grew to its present size by absorbing Grove Labs, the Drackett Co. (*Drano*, *Windex*), and *Clairol*. A recent CBS study showed that only 33 advertisers in the U.S. had the resources to underwrite the costs of a half-hour network series. Freedom in the marketplace steadily declines, even among its industrial participants.

The solution lies not in the halls of Congress but in industry. "The free enterprise system," Betty Furness said in an address to the American Trial Lawyers association in July, 1968, "has no better protector than the consumer who knows that competition gives him more choice and, ideally, a quality and price comparison, and who shops around to find the best buy. Unless we as a nation acknowledge this, and act to give consumers equal bargaining power and recourse in law, I think, we substantially weaken our free enterprise system. . ."

An Equal Contest

chapter 10

American industry gets the credit for the past successes of the consumer revolution—first, by falling down on the job of taking care of its customers, and then by steadfastly refusing to see what all the fuss was about. In all, industry's views in the decade of the consumer have been the most misguided since John D. Rockefeller said that "God gave me my money."

If any further evidence is necessary, the truth-in-packaging act is an example. It was born at the breakfast table of Senator Philip Hart, when he discovered that his family's favorite cereal, *Nabisco Shredded Wheat*, was in a new package. The package was taller, the price was the same, and the contents were reduced by 1¾ ounces. The bill was kept alive across six years by the packaging industry. Early in 1967, *Fortune* observed: "Industry's strategic mistake in battling truth in packaging was to adopt an attitude of intransigent opposition. The companies denied any need for the bill, challenged the right of the Federal government to interfere, and attempted to kill the legislation. They thereby lost a number of opportunities to come to terms with Congress on an early compromise. Five years of lengthy public hearings gave consumerists a public forum for publicizing their cause and complaints. If 'consumerism' is really 'rampant,' then the companies that stock the nation's supermarkets helped make it that way."

The same behavior pattern was still in evidence right up to the end of the 1968 legislative session. A massive lobbying job had brought the poultry-inspection bill to the brink of defeat. The Senate Agriculture Committee had been won over. So had

the United States Department of Agriculture, which Abraham
Lincoln had created and labeled "the people's department."
Senator Spessard Holland of Florida had introduced an amendment that would have made the situation worse than before the
bill had been introduced; he wanted states to retain the
inspection role, and to give their local chicken processors the
right to ship their wares through interstate commerce without
Federal inspection. It took a last-minute effort by the White
House, Senators Joseph Montoya and Walter Mondale, and a
six-day lobbying job by Ralph Nader to kill the Holland proposal.

The fight for meaningful controls over X-radiation was
advanced when Nader dug out a study done by California health
officials, which showed that of 90 X-ray technicians interviewed,
72 routinely gave heavier doses to Negroes in the belief that their
bones were more dense and difficult to penetrate. The American
College of Radiologists instantly counterattacked, saying there
was no medical basis for any such thing, and calling the report
inaccurate and "malicious." The attack on Nader's credibility
went on for days.

The time might better have been spent in some quiet
checking. A few days later, officials of the Department of Health,
Education and Welfare reported that they had made similar
findings. New York health officials confirmed that the extra dose
for Negroes was common practice. California officials confirmed
Nader's report. General Electric instruction manuals as recently as
1964 advised just such procedure. Finally, an X-ray technician
textbook was produced which confidently stated that the extra
dose was necessary. A strong bill passed.

In the middle of the battle over gas-pipeline safety, a gas
distribution line exploded in Richmond, Indiana, killed 44
people, injuring more than 100, causing $30 million in damage. In
Atlanta, 10 children were killed when leaking gas blew up a
school. Yet the quiet and effective lobbying job against the bill
went on without a hitch. Senator Warren Magnuson finally took
charge, rolled over the opposition with facts and logic. The bill
passed in reasonably good shape.

The response of Dr. Robert S. Long, head of the American
Society for Internal Medicine, to continuing efforts to police the
safety and effectiveness of drugs, was the following statement
quoted in *U.S. Medicine*: "I don't pay much heed to all this

scientific testing, this measurement of blood levels, this testing in animals. I am accustomed to certain brands, and I have good luck with them. The final test is the patient himself. If I want to know if a drug is any good or not, I ask my patients."

Of such stuff is the consumer movement made.

If industry's attitude has heated up the consumer movement, then it follows that industry's attitude could also cool it down in the future. Indeed it could. On the legislative front alone, it would be a relatively simple matter. When a piece of legislation looms, a realistic assessment of the problems that generated it, rather than automatic insistence that everything is all right, would work wonders. Once hearings begin, industry can provide its own considerable expertise and offer a range of possible solutions. Such a response would lead to a useful dialogue, rather than the traditional argument, and would also avoid creation of the massive industrial credibility gap which eventually appeared in virtually all past battles. If lines of communication are kept open right up to the end, the end will come sooner, headlines will be fewer, and the reputation of industry will be cleaner. The laws that finally pass with industry's cooperation are liable to be far better than ones pushed through over the shouts of a few panicked lobbyists fighting for their jobs.

Here and there, industry voices have suggested to their colleagues that the techniques of the past have been wrong. Howard Bell, president of the American Advertising Federation, told his colleagues at a 1968 meeting: ". . .my own conclusions about the Washington environment, the government and the people who run it, are these: government people are generally accessible, most of them are reasonable. They respond to well-made cases, quietly presented, based on facts and research. They are interested in explanations of the unanticipated effects of some of their proposals. Often they accept suggestions designed to correct, limit, or make more precise those actions. Generally they do *not* respond to shouting and abuse, flag-waving, constitution crackling and empty rhetoric. Stone wall opposition to anything and everything provokes ultimately stone deaf response to your pleas. You simply lose all credentials as a credible voice in Washington."

Some, unfortunately, interpret such advice to mean that the new tactic should be to halt frontal warfare in favor of wheeling Trojan horses into Senate hearing rooms. Kind offers to help overworked committee staffers edit the bill are often nothing more than guerrilla tactics, with the ultimate motive of sabotaging the whole operation. Sometimes the tactic works, but usually it backfires and further polarizes relations between Washington and industry. Hopefully Mr. Bell did not mean that. His suggestion is to find a middle ground, an area of voluntary compromise and joint effort.

Legislation could in many cases be headed off completely by a change of attitude in the hearing room. But that requires change of attitude in the boardroom. "Will Business Ever Seize the Social Initiative?" an *Ad Age* column by E.B. Weiss was headlined. He thought yes. Said Weiss: "The era of industry's automatic resistance to government. . .has barely begun to wane. But I am sufficiently optimistic to conclude that simultaneously with this waning opposition there will emerge this new form of competition, a race to lead competitors in the development of more 'socially responsible products,' a whole new concept."

The essential point to be weighed by industry is that there are more considerations involved in a product than its salability. As a corollary, there is more involved in selling a product than a clever ad campaign. The prime motivation of the consumer movement is a desire that business crank into its marketplace equations the social costs of its actions. Far from a vague and naive wish, the concept of social costs takes many very specific and realistic forms. For one, it means following a product all the way from the end of the assembly line to the home of the purchaser. Too often the middleman is really caught in the middle, between a consumer seeking redress and a company ignoring its responsibility. The doctrine of privity has been denied many times over in the nation's courts; no matter how many hands a product passes through on the way to its final sale, the line of responsibility reaches back to its point of origin.

Safety is another obvious social cost. The price the nation pays in money and time lost, and in anguish, from avoidable injuries is unacceptable. Many industries are on the verge of becoming prisoners of the problem of danger and its consequences. The lack of self-policing in the drug industry has forced government to fill the vacuum. An air-traffic control network, by contrast, is left completely up to the government; with inadequate funds, personnel and research, the system is strangling the nation's airlines with delays, inefficiencies, and occasional tragedies. The insurance system that should provide a legal framework for the auto industry's products is inundating the courts to the point where justice has become an empty word.

Another social cost not so easily computed is the questionable need, desire, and purpose of new products. Up to a point, competition between similar products can lead to innovation and progress. Beyond that point, competition becomes unproductive for all involved. When a market is saturated and all wants are met for a certain type of product, it becomes a difficult exercise to justify the reasons for introducing another carbon copy. The only motive for marketing an imitation is sales, to be gained by stealing a chunk of the market away from the competition by virtue of a heavy advertising and marketing campaign. For industry as a whole, the end result is a mob of manufacturers running to stay in the same place, with competition driving prices to unreasonable levels. The cosmetics industry is a prime example. No consumer advocate objects to the number of lipstick colors on the market. It is the prices that a few cents worth of beeswax, perfume and color command that raises eyebrows. Sometimes prices are raised as a sales gimmick to make the product seem better than it is.

One particularly exasperating social cost of industry's actions is the steadily lowering quality of its wares. More letters by far arrive in Washington complaining of product defects than any other subject. Among the flag-waving phrases such as free enterprise and freedom of competition that industry trots out to justify the status quo, one that is seldom heard anymore is "pride of workmanship." Some say it has been supplanted by deliberately contrived shoddiness.

Elisha Gray II, Whirlpool Corporation board chairman, stated it this way: "An engineer's principal purpose as an engineer is to create obsolescence. Any attempts by various people to toady up to the public by saying they are against planned obsolescence is so much commercial demagogy." Taken at its most charitable interpretation, Mr. Gray's comment was apparently meant to discourage his colleagues from making unjustified claims for their products.

The phrase "planned obsolescence" is somewhat of a misconception. A good engineer does indeed set out to make current products obsolete by designing better ones. That is called progress. And in a field whose technology is rapidly evolving, it is unwise to build extra long life (which the consumer must pay for) into a product. There is also a crossover point between quality and cost; a Mercedes is a far better engineered vehicle than any American car, but not that many people are willing or able to pay the price.

But when an appliance manufacturer rearranges the dials and buttons on his machine and declares all earlier versions obsolete, or deliberately underengineers his product to keep sales volume high, the phrase takes on true meaning. The only proper justification for obsolescence is progress.

There is a good deal of mystery connected with the inability of industry to respond to these problems. Some point to the corporate institution and maintain that it is hidebound and oversized. Others point to the lack of communications not only between the corporation heads and their customers, but also within the organization. Still others suggest that large corporations are, by their nature, innovation-stifling institutions.

There is much evidence to support all these beliefs. Fundamentally, the issue is whether size is compatible with progress. It probably is. But it hasn't been in the past. Autos are self-starting nowadays, but the automakers aren't. The safety advances in American auto design made since the days of the *Model T* wouldn't fill a full-page ad. But once goaded into action over protestations that retooling takes years and costs millions, the industry built devices such as collapsible steering columns into autos within months. Now the list of safety features already in or on the way would make quite a respectable list. Many were copied from European manufacturers, but many others were generated by engineers who, once given authority to innovate, produced in fine style.

The problem with the corporation is never capability, but intention. Giving an engineer a free hand and a solid line of communication with the company's policy-makers costs nothing. The problem is that big corporations inevitably subdivide into dozens of mini-empires, innovation-stifling unions included, all arranged in an elaborate pecking order, and the whole structure becomes so rigid that it takes a few mortar rounds from Washington to shake it into change. It is safe to say that Ford, GM, or Chrysler could easily have designed a practical steam-driven car that would dramatically reduce air pollution in the nation. But they didn't; two brothers from Pennsylvania did. Despite all the corporate capability in printing, photography, and electronics, xerography was developed in an apartment in Astoria, Long Island, and finally peddled to the Establishment after years of passionate disinterest in the idea. New ideas seldom come from institutions, from the Establishment.

The lexicon and actions of the Establishment reveal its awareness of the problem. Talk about "clearing out the deadwood," and "bringing in new blood" sweeps through every corporation periodically. Outside management consultants are brought in from time to time to get the corporate pulsebeat going again. In the end though, little comes of it; the most common means of giving a corporation a new challenge or a new direction is to buy out a small company with an innovation to sell. It is much simpler for a corporation to grow than to evolve.

But now the pressures to evolve are becoming irresistible. All the Establishments are under pressure. The Church has its young priests, the Democratic party had its Senator Eugene McCarthy, the Soviet Union has Czechoslovakia, and industry has its consumer movement. The call in all cases is for reform, and the consumer's call is for corporate reform. Industry even has another Establishment pushing it—the Federal government.

The disaffection with the corporate system is an aftereffect of the easy affluence it has generated; a society variously described as post-industrial or post-material is in the process of creation. It looks past mere acquisition to the quality of the acquisition and the price paid for them not merely in dollars but also in social costs. It is difficult to believe that industry couldn't join the movement past the acquisitive society to the inquisitive society, and begin questioning its own role in American life.

Whatever the imagined penalties of change might be, the price of no movement at all threatens to be much higher. Senator Warren Magnuson has spoken of the danger of "legislative overkill." Unyielding opposition to needed change closes all options to the government except for corrective and punitive legislation. There are already some legislative proposals loose in

Washington which threaten to carry change too far in the other direction. The chronic lack of product information has generated interest in a Federal product-rating service, or a national data bank of consumer information. One powerful proponent is Senator Philip Hart. "Thus far," he said in August, 1968, "the consumer movement has been either making minor adjustments in major consumer areas or major adjustments in minor consumer areas. The time is ripe now for major adjustments to major problems." He promised to introduce a bill calling for a consumer service foundation that would rate products according to the results of government tests, and disseminate the information by means of a computerized vending machine system.

Heretofore, the government has contented itself with regularizing the marketplace by setting standards and creating uniform guidelines. But a proposal such as Senator Hart's involves direct participation by the government in the marketplace—not in any uniform way but product by product. By definition, the process is a discriminatory one, based on the judgments of human beings in a government lab.

The possibilities for corruption are infinite. As one critic of the plan observed: "A $10,000 bribe is still cheaper than a one-minute spot on the Johnny Carson Show." The possibilities for argument are also endless; there are limits on objectivity in rating products. Different consumers look for different things in their purchases. *Consumer Reports'* ratings take varying needs and tastes into account by means of long articles preceding the ratings, and a capsule explanation of the reasons behind each product's rating. And still, it is inevitable that what pleases the raters may not please the buyers.

But the proposal is a revealing index to the exasperation present in Washington with the state of the marketplace today—and if the marketplace doesn't make repairs, Washington will. Industry's response will either be to dig in its heels and call the plan communism or socialism, or to acknowledge that the lack of information in the marketplace is epidemic and see what it can do. A voluntary compromise, for example patterned on the European "teltag" system of uniform, and informative, labeling of all goods, might emerge, with the government playing the role of light-handed overseer. The proper role of government in the marketplace is as rule-maker, referee, and final arbiter, not as decision-maker.

Another proposal bound to be given strong consideration is the suggestion that a cabinet-level Department of Consumer Affairs be formed. The purpose of creating the consumer's own agency would be to give the cause more visibility, more power. But others, many consumer advocates included, doubt the wisdom of this course. The last thing the government needs is another bureaucracy. The intention of the Johnson Administration, in fact, was to head in the other direction, cut down bureaucracy, and realign the government along more functional lines. The President was largely unable to carry out his intention, except for forming the Department of Transportation out of a collection of offices spread all over town. His State of the Union proposal to merge the Commerce and Labor Departments into one Department of Business and Labor was shot down by the instant and overwhelming opposition of the labor movement.

The purpose, though, was to merge two functions that in the end dealt with the same field—the operation of the American industrial machine. In the same sense, creating a separate consumer office ignores realities—most cabinet agencies must concern themselves with the consumer, from Agriculture to Commerce to the Department of Defense (GI's are consumers, too). The better idea is to keep the responsibility where the expertise is. To coordinate and catalyze action on the part of the consumer, the simplest and best idea seems to be to have an office in the White House separate from the cabinet empires. This office can act as an executive oversight agency, and exert its influence through the President directly, and through inter-departmental meetings. This, of course, is exactly the structure that exists now. Enforcement of approved legislation properly belongs in the appropriate agency, most of which could raise consumer affairs to the level of an assistant secretaryship to give it more visibility and more power within each agency's bureaucratic structure. The Presidential adviser, meanwhile, acts as the cutting edge of the movement, listening to the consumer's complaints and industry's responses, proposing, suggesting, cajoling, and recommending legislation to the President if need be.

How fast and how far the government carries the consumer movement depends to a degree on the political coloration in Washington in the next few years. But whatever the political atmosphere is, the social climate is not likely to change. This is a time of change in all arenas. Both foreign and domestic policy are in ferment. The focal points of power within the government are shifting, the power structure within the private sectors of society is being redesigned. The society is evolving, and the economy and its practitioners are evolving along with it. The move is toward more voice for the invisible, the ignored, and the disenchanted sectors of the nation. The move would worry an Alexander Hamilton, but make a Thomas Jefferson cheer. The evolution has its excesses and its errors, but the direction is up. The end is a greater degree of freedom on all fronts, and hopefully the more responsible exercise of the traditional freedoms that American industry enjoys.

Betty Furness put it this way to the American Bar Association: "I hope the past has taught us much and that a new era of consumer relations will be achieved without hammering out such a code over the piled up bodies of the defenders of the status quo."

Index